MANAGING PROJECTS
A WORLD OF PEOPLE,
STRATEGY AND CHANGE

Project management is at a crossroads: There is a pressing need to rethink the approaches used in initiating, managing and governing projects, programmes and change initiatives. The aim of this book is to progress the dialogue around project practice by shifting the focus from instrumental methods and prescriptive techniques towards a context-sensitive consideration of people, strategy and change.

Projects are initiated to deliver agreed outputs that can be translated into meaningful outcomes capable of satisfying the wishes and expectations for improvement and development. Yet, people, strategy and change, which are largely ignored by the conventional bodies of knowledge, are clearly central to the sustainable and enduring success of projects, efforts and initiatives.

The volume brings together some of the best writing by leading authorities on key topics including trust, ethics, people, psychology, requirements, project performance, audits, uncertainty, anti-fragility, strategic initiatives, governance, change management and commercial management. The collection offers an invaluable new resource for informed managers looking to engage with the latest thinking and research.

Darren Dalcher is Honorary Professor of Project Management at the University of Kent. He has written over 200 papers and book chapters and published over 30 books. He is Editor-in-Chief of the *Journal of Software: Evolution and Process* and of two established book series published by Routledge.

Advances in Project Management
Edited by Darren Dalcher

Project management has become a key competence for most organisations in the public and private sectors. Driven by recent business trends such as fewer management layers, greater flexibility, increasing geographical distribution and more project-based work, project management has grown beyond its roots in the construction, engineering and aerospace industries to transform the service, financial, computer, and general management sectors. In fact, a Fortune article rated project management as the number one career choice at the beginning of the 21st century. Yet many organizations have struggled in applying the traditional models of project management to their new projects in the global environment.

Project management offers a framework to help organisations to transform their mainstream operations and service performance. It is viewed as a way of organising for the future. Moreover, in an increasingly busy, stressful, and uncertain world it has become necessary to manage several projects successfully at the same time. According to some estimates the world annually spends well over $10 trillion (US) on projects. In the UK alone, more than £250 billion is spent on projects every year. Up to half of these projects fail! A major ingredient in the build-up leading to failure is often cited as the lack of adequate project management knowledge and experience. Some organizations have responded to this situation by trying to improve the understanding and capability of their managers and employees who are introduced to projects, as well as their experienced project managers in an attempt to enhance their competence and capability in this area.

Advances in Project Management provides short, state of play, guides to the main aspects of the new emerging applications including: maturity models, agile projects, extreme projects, six sigma and projects, human factors and leadership in projects, project governance, value management, virtual teams, project benefits.

For a complete list of titles in this series, please visit https://www.routledge.com/business/series/APM

Managing Projects in a World of People, Strategy and Change
Edited by Darren Dalcher

The Evolution of Project Management Practice
From Programmes and Contracts to Benefits and Change
Edited by Darren Dalcher

Further Advances in Project Management
Guided Exploration in/of Unfamiliar Landscapes
Edited by Darren Dalcher

Net Present Value and Risk Modelling for Projects
By Martin Hopkinson

MANAGING PROJECTS IN A WORLD OF PEOPLE, STRATEGY AND CHANGE

Edited by Darren Dalcher

Routledge
Taylor & Francis Group

LONDON AND NEW YORK

First published 2019
by Routledge
2 Park Square, Milton Park, Abingdon, Oxon OX14 4RN

and by Routledge
711 Third Avenue, New York, NY 10017

Routledge is an imprint of the Taylor & Francis Group, an informa business

British Library Cataloguing-in-Publication Data
A catalogue record for this book is available from the British Library

Library of Congress Cataloging-in-Publication Data
Names: Dalcher, Darren, editor.
Title: Managing projects in a world of people, strategy and change / edited
by Darren Dalcher.
Description: 1 Edition. | New York : Routledge, 2019. | Series: Advances
in project management | Includes bibliographical references and index.
Identifiers: LCCN 2018018285 (print) | LCCN 2018020111 (ebook) |
ISBN 9780429449741 (eBook) | ISBN 9781138326606 (hardback : alk.
paper) | ISBN 9781138326637 (pbk. : alk. paper)
Subjects: LCSH: Project management.
Classification: LCC HD69.P75 (ebook) | LCC HD69.P75 M36344 2019
(print) | DDC 658.4/04–dc23
LC record available at https://lccn.loc.gov/2018018285

ISBN: 9781138326606 (hbk)
ISBN: 9781138326637 (pbk)
ISBN: 9780429449741 (ebk)

Typeset in Bembo
by Florence Production Ltd, Stoodleigh, Devon

CONTENTS

FIGURES AND TABLES

Figures

Tables

ABOUT THE EDITOR

Darren Dalcher is Honorary Professor of Project Management at the University of Kent and holds visiting appointments at Warwick Manufacturing Group, Drexel University, SKEMA Business School, Vienna University of Economics and Business, and the University of Iceland. He is the founder and Director of the National Centre for Project Management (NCPM), an interdisciplinary centre of excellence operating in collaboration with industry, government, academia, third sector organisations and the learned societies.

Following industrial and consultancy experience in managing technology projects, Professor Dalcher gained his PhD from King's College London for his work on continuous delivery, dynamic feedback and extended software project cycles. In 1992, he founded an IEEE taskforce focused on learning from project failures. He is active in numerous international committees, standards bodies, steering groups and editorial boards. He is heavily involved in organising international conferences, and has delivered many international keynote addresses and tutorials. He has written over 200 refereed papers and book chapters and published over 30 books. His work has been translated into French, German, Spanish, Italian, Russian and Portuguese. He is Editor-in-Chief of Wiley's *Journal of Software: Evolution and Process* and of two established book series focused on managing projects and change initiatives published by Routledge.

He has built a reputation as leader and innovator in the area of practice-based education and reflection in project management and has designed, developed and launched the UK's first professional doctorate in project management, alongside an extensive suite of executive and professional master's programmes and diplomas. In 2008 he was named by the Association for Project Management as one of the top ten influential experts in project management and has also been voted Project Magazine's Academic of the Year for his contribution in 'integrating and weaving academic work with practice'. He has been chairman of the influential APM Project Management Conference for an unprecedented five years, expanding the scope and content of the event, setting consecutive attendance records and bringing together the most influential speakers.

He received international recognition in 2010 with his appointment as a member of the PMForum International Academic Advisory Council. In October 2011 he was awarded a prestigious lifetime Honorary Fellowship from the Association for Project Management for outstanding contribution to the discipline of project management.

He has delivered lectures and courses in many institutions across Europe and North America and has won multiple awards and prizes, including most recently, the 2015 Best Paper Award from the British Academy of Management, the 2016 CMI's Management Articles of the Year competition and a 2017 Outstanding Paper Award in the Emerald Literati Network Awards for Excellence. His research interests focus on rethinking project success and project agility, as well as maturity and capability; process improvement; systems engineering; decision making; change management; ethics; complexity; project leadership; knowledge management; and reflective practice.

Professor Dalcher is an Honorary Fellow of the Association for Project Management, a Chartered Fellow of the British Computer Society, a Senior Fellow of the Higher Education Academy, a Fellow of the Chartered Management Institute, and of the Royal Society of Arts, a Senior Member of the IEEE and a Member of the Project Management Institute and of the Academy of Management. He sits on numerous senior research and professional boards, including the PMI Academic Member Advisory Group, the APM Research Advisory Group, the International Advisory Council of PM World Today, the CMI Academic Council and the APM Group Ethics and Standards Governance Board.

Darren Dalcher Ph.D. (Lond) HonFAPM FCMI
FRSA FBCS CITP SMIEEE SFHEA

NOTES ON CONTRIBUTORS

Tony Bendell is a respected academic and international expert on improvement. Tony is a well-known invited speaker at conferences worldwide, and was formerly the Rolls-Royce-funded Professor of Quality Management at the University of Leicester, UK. A leading figure in quality and productivity improvement and excellence, he has published extensively and is principal author of the bestselling Financial Times book on Benchmarking, available in six languages. Professor Bendell also has extensive international knowledge of the field of Lean & Six Sigma. This has been added to by Professor Bendell's unique experience as chair of BSI Technical Committee MS6, which developed the new ISO18404:2015 certifiable Lean & Six Sigma international standard, and his current role as project manager of the sector scheme set up by the Royal Statistical Society in cooperation with the major UKAS accredited certification bodies to allow accredited certification against ISO18404.

Nicola Busby is an experienced business change professional who is passionate about the benefits that business change management can bring to organisations and staff going through change. She has supported many organisations in the private, public and non-profit sectors through a wide variety of change, including: organisational transformations, restructures and mergers, IT-enabled change, cultural and behavioural change, building organisational capacity to deliver change. Nicola's clients have included Penguin Random House, Houses of Parliament, Financial Ombudsman Service, National Childbirth Trust, BBC, ITV, Network Rail and Kent County Council. Nicola is an accredited trainer for the APMG Change Management qualification, and authored a chapter on 'Change Readiness, Planning and Measurement' for the set text for the course *The Effective Change Manager's Handbook*.

Terry Cooke-Davies has been a practitioner of both general and project management since the end of the 1960s and a consultant to blue-chip organisations for over 20 years. He was the founder and Executive Chairman of Human Systems International, a global consulting firm which assesses the excellence of organisations' project, programme and portfolio management capability, and operates a leading-edge knowledge management network. With a PhD in Project Management, a bachelor's degree in Theology and qualifications in electrical engineering, management accounting and counselling, Terry has worked alongside senior leaders and managers in both the public and the private sectors to ensure the delivery of business-critical change programmes and enhance the quality of leadership. He is co-author with Paul C. Dinsmore of *The Right Projects, Done Right*, published by Jossey-Bass in October 2005.

Robin Hornby graduated from Queens University Belfast with a degree in aeronautical engineering and a master's in applied science. Robin's career began with IBM United Kingdom as systems engineer. Moving to Canada in 1977, he worked in the telecommunications sector as systems planner before embarking on his project management career with DMR Consulting. In 1995 he was offered the role of National Delivery Manager for Intergraph Canada, and in a few years returned the service's business to profitability. This role continued following the establishment of Tempest Management Inc. (TMI) in 1997, which allowed the pursuit of wider interests, including a ten-year affiliation with Mount Royal University to teach the PMBOK" curriculum and collaborate in the development and delivery of custom courses for corporate clients. Robin is the author of three books. Recent consulting assignments have included project risk reviews, contract reviews, project management (PM) coaching and delivery and project office management roles. His current focus is on writing and conducting seminars on the aspects of project management which he believes are neglected – commercial practice, methodology for collaborative procurement of services and PM leadership to achieve project quality.

Ngaire E. Hunt commenced her career in nursing and qualified as a New Zealand Registered Nurse. She then worked as a Registered Nurse in New Zealand and the UK, before returning to New Zealand and moving into management of nursing services. In 2008 she shifted her career to project management and worked, primarily in health-related fields, as a project manager in New Zealand until 2015. In 2015 she moved to Australia and, since then, has been working as a project manager in a health-related consultancy in Melbourne. She holds her PMP qualification.

Douglas G. Long teaches values, ethics and leadership at the School of Business, University of New South Wales, Sydney. From 1988 to 2000 he was associated with Macquarie Graduate School of Management in Sydney, where he researched, designed and delivered the programme Leadership in Senior Management. His latest book (with Zivit Inbar), *The Ethical Kaleidoscope: Values, Ethics, and Corporate Governance*, has just (2017) been released by Routledge. Two of his previous books, *Delivering High Performance: The Third Generation Organisation* and *Third Generation Leadership and the Locus of Control: Knowledge, Change and Neuroscience*, were published by Gower. For the past 40 years he has been teaching, consulting and public speaking in Australia, New Zealand, Papua New Guinea, South East Asia, Europe and the USA. He holds the degree of PhD in Organisational Psychology.

Alexia Nalewaik is a project controls director and management consultant with 25 years of experience in the industry. She is President-Elect 2017–2018 of AACE International, Research Chair and Past-Chair of the International Cost Engineering Council and the owner of QS Requin Corporation. She holds a PhD in Project and Programme Management, an MS in Structural Engineering, and a BA in Physics. Alexia is a certified cost professional, a certified construction auditor and a chartered quantity surveyor. She is a Fellow of AACE International, RICS and ICEC.

Martin Samphire is the owner and Managing Director of 3pmxl Ltd, a consultancy that is based in the UK and specialises in implementing major transformation and helping clients to transform their business using structured PPPM approaches. He has over 30 years of management consulting, change, project, programme and portfolio implementation experience in both the private and public sectors – in the UK and internationally. He has directed and contributed to a number of complex business and organisational change programmes to fundamentally reshape and improve client business performance, often enabled by technology. He has also led a number of assignments to improve an organisation's capability to better manage portfolios, projects and programmes. Martin is a mechanical engineer by training and started his career in major capital project contracting in the petrochemical sector with Foster Wheeler. He moved into consulting with The Nichols Group and thence to Impact Plus and Hitachi Consulting, helping organisations to implement organisational change in a more structured project- and programme-oriented way. He started 3pmxl in 2011. Martin is Chairman of the UK-based Association for Project Management (APM) Specific Interest Group (SIG) on Governance.

Fred Voskoboynikov worked as an industrial psychologist in a civil engineering firm and taught ergonomics at Civil Engineering University in Odessa, Ukraine. He developed a course on psychological methods of management and gave related lectures and seminars to managers of industrial firms and organisations of Odessa and the Odessa region. He is an Honorary Professor of Psychology at Baltic Academy of Education (St Petersburg, Russia) and a regular contributor to the Academy's periodic journal. Since immigrating to the United States he has worked as a manager of construction projects in the San Francisco Bay Area. He has combined his work with writing on the psychology of management, the psychology of individual differences and on some theoretical issues. His writings have been published by Taylor and Francis Group in the proceedings of International Conferences on Applied Human Factors and Ergonomics and in collections of articles. His most recent book, *The Psychology of Effective Management: Strategies for Relationship Building*, was published by Routledge in 2017.

PM World Journal

The *PM World Journal* (*PMWJ*) is an online publication produced by PM World Inc. in the United States, but created by a virtual team of advisors, correspondents and contributing editors located worldwide. Each month, the *PMWJ* features dozens of new articles, papers and stories about programmes, projects and project management (P/PM) around the world. Objectives for the journal are to (1) support the creation of new P/PM knowledge; (2) support the transfer of that knowledge to individuals, organisations and locations where professional P/PM may be weak, less available or sorely needed; (3) provide recognition and visibility for authors, the creators of new P/PM knowledge; (4) provide an easily accessible and useful online repository of P/PM knowledge and information as a global resource for knowledge sharing and continuous learning; and (5) promote the application of modern, professional P/PM for solving more of the world's problems – to make this world a better place.

INTRODUCTION: THE CHALLENGE OF CHANGE: IDENTIFYING NEW AND IMPROVED THEORIES FOR PROJECT MANAGEMENT

Darren Dalcher

> Change can be frightening, and the temptation is often to resist it. But change almost always provides opportunities – to learn new things, to rethink tired processes, and to improve the way we work.
>
> Klaus Martin Schwab

Welcome to another title in the *Advances in Project Management* series. This volume endeavours to help practitioners by focusing on key areas emphasising capabilities, skills, attitudes, values and competencies that are required in order to successfully deliver projects, especially in increasingly change-ridden environments.

Some of the published statistics on project performance appear to convey a dismal track record on delivery. Anecdotal stories of failure seem to suggest that in the rush to deliver projects according to their initially imposed constraints, stakeholders, needs, potential uses and impacts often get ignored, leaving the deliverables in an unused or unusable state. Other projects struggle to sell the change or make it stick, fail to consider the strategic organisational agenda, priorities and needs, or simply ignore the benefits, considerations or expectations identified in the business case.

Project management is at a crossroads: There is a pressing need to rethink the approaches used in initiating, managing and governing projects, programmes and change initiatives. The aim of this book is to progress the dialogue around project practice by shifting the focus from instrumental methods and techniques towards a context-sensitive consideration of people, strategy and change.

Projects are initiated to deliver agreed outputs that can be translated into meaningful outcomes capable of satisfying the wishes and expectations for improvement, growth and development. Yet, people, strategy and change, which are largely ignored by the conventional bodies of knowledge, are clearly central to the sustainable and enduring success of projects, efforts and initiatives.

While there is a plethora of new publications and books focused on project management, we recognise that it can sometimes be difficult to know where to look and what to follow. Finding a starting point can be difficult. Moreover, identifying key concepts and ideas, especially in new domains, is time consuming and labour intensive. This volume therefore offers a sample of some of the best writing centred on projects, people, strategy and change.

The content is divided into nine main areas. Each area is explored from two distinct perspectives. First, an introductory narrative sets the scene and explains the context, typically focusing on the key ideas, main thinkers or revisiting seminal writing. The areas explored often borrow from other disciplines or perspectives, and the writing tries to address an important question, explore paradoxes or review progress to date. Second, the main guest-authored chapter features new ideas, ways of thinking or perspectives. Readers are strongly encouraged to pursue the additional sources listed in the chapters, which can offer further insight and detail. The seminal works indicated in the introductory narrative are also worth pursuing. (Note: chapter 3 deviates from the more standard format by offering a primer, or a tutorial, on project requirements management – a much misunderstood area).

The chapters in this collection bring together leading authorities on topics that are relevant to managing, leading and directing projects. Topics include trust, ethics, people, psychology, requirements, project performance, audits, uncertainty, anti-fragility, strategic initiatives, governance, change management and commercial management.

The volume offers an introduction to a range of both brand new and established ideas. It also introduces different perspectives and ways of thinking, as well as a host of new writers, thinkers and scholars from other domains and areas. The main aims of the collection are to reflect on and summarise the state of practice, to propose new extensions and additions to existing practice, to distil new insights and to provide a way of sampling a range of the most promising ideas, perspectives, approaches, perspectives and styles of writing from leading thinkers and practitioners.

Change is an opportunity to reflect

Project management ought to be simple. It would be tempting to settle for a set of processes and procedures for managing projects as they help us to perform tasks more skilfully. Reducing skills into a set of procedures is particularly appealing from a teaching or training perspective as it offers a natural structure that can be translated into a lesson plan, or a development plan, and ultimately pared down to a set of steps to be memorised and mastered.

However, in reality we all know that the craft and discipline of project management cannot be simplified and reduced to chunks of knowledge. The skills, behaviours and interactions of successful project managers rely on understanding the complex interplay between people, organisations and change. Lessons from project failures have taught us to take heed of relationships, expectations, trust, communication, politics, conflict and even human follies and imperfections.

The challenge for reflective practitioners is in how to develop the new capabilities and responses required for success. Capabilities integrate skills, knowledge, attitudes and perspectives with our emerging understanding. But capabilities also extend beyond the familiar context, pointing towards the uncertainty of new and changing circumstances.

In order to succeed in an uncertain and change-riddled environment, we need to recognise the value of capabilities over repeatable procedures. Being capable therefore is not about responding to the present by repeating the past but is, rather, about grappling with the unknown and unfamiliar so that we can begin to imagine the future and bring it about.

Schwab's characterisation of change (see the quote at the beginning of this introduction) acknowledges the potential embedded in confrontations with change. It implies that looking backwards and repeating past solutions and approaches offers limited value when faced with new conditions, uncertainty and innovation. Terms such as 'uberisation' are increasingly used to describe situations where an entire industry is turned on its head when a new technology, such as technology platforms and networked markets, can force a fundamental rethink of how things are done within a sector. Fundamental challenges question the validity of the models, assumptions and operating modes, introducing the potential for transformational change to how things are done. Other change is more gradual and evolutionary, delivering a slow and steady adaptation to shared practice.

Learning is a product of experience. Many project practitioners who live in dynamic and change-infused environments embark on discovery journeys precisely because they are struggling to understand elements of the real world. Many endeavour to make sense of their environment with theories and procedures that seem ineffective in dealing with the unfamiliar. When the theory fails to make sense of experiences they discover a disconnect – or ignore the experience.

Renowned educational theorist David Kolb (2014) has noted that learning is a process whereby knowledge is created through the transformation of experience. Learning is therefore an active process of interacting, questioning, reconciling and making sense. Kolb's Learning Cycle explains how experience is reflected upon, before conclusions are drawn and knowledge reorganised, to enable learners to use their new knowledge and continue to make sense of the unfamiliar world (Figure 0.1).

Learning and development take place through the active attempt to solve a problem. In an imperfect and unfamiliar world, knowledge and action need to follow one another in a cycle of contemplation, reflection and application (Dalcher, 2014). When we recognise imperfections and unfamiliarity, action begins to create new opportunities for learning that we must grasp. Playwright and author T. S. Eliot once wrote, 'We had the experience but missed the meaning.' We can create meaning by digesting our experiences, reflecting on the outcomes and making sense of our actions.

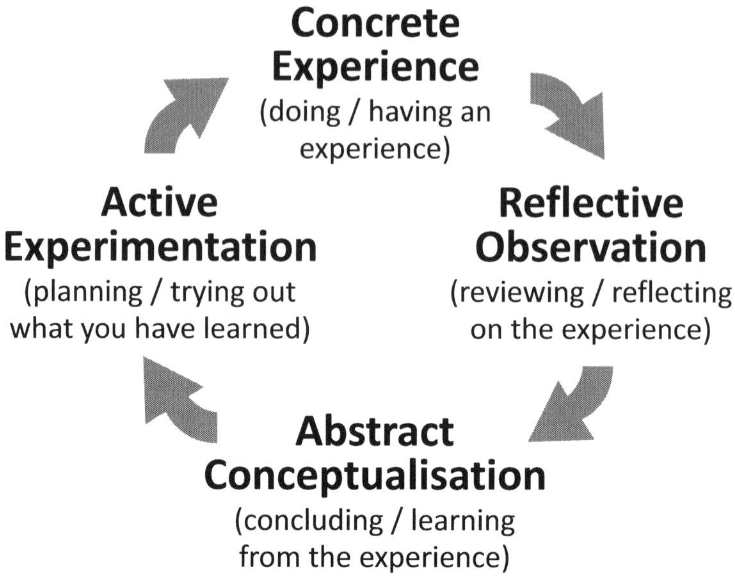

Concrete Experience
(doing / having an experience)

Active Experimentation
(planning / trying out what you have learned)

Reflective Observation
(reviewing / reflecting on the experience)

Abstract Conceptualisation
(concluding / learning from the experience)

FIGURE 0.1 Kolb's Learning Cycle

Practitioners grappling, trying to make sense of context and unexpected results, must begin by recognising that they are adrift without a permanent theory to grasp onto. They are then ready to reflect and challenge the underlying theory of project management . . .

Where is the theory of project management?

There have been many debates about the extent, role, nature and existence of underpinning theory in project management. Theory appears to play a key, if subtle, role in defining both knowledge and practice. Indeed, Albert Einstein opined that 'it is the theory which decides what we can observe'.

Project practice meanwhile has been subjected to a multitude of failure and success surveys, often revealing that the state of practice is some way from being adequate. If we accept that methods do not simply describe, but also help to create the social worlds, we can begin to question the nature of our interaction with theory through intermediate artefacts.

The Oxford Dictionary defines theory as either a set of ideas formulated to explain something; an opinion or supposition; or a statement of principles on which a subject is based. Many professions seek to build a theoretical body of knowledge to underpin, explain and support professional judgement. Bodies of knowledge, such as the Association of Project Managers' *Body of Knowledge* (APM BoK) can satisfy the latter definition by offering a selective grouping of conceptual principles and normative assertions that are said to apply to a discipline or profession. Indeed,

Sibeon (1991) notes that one of recognised hallmarks of a profession is a body of specialist knowledge, which acts as the basis for professional expertise.

According to Koskela and Howell (2002), an explicit theory of project management would serve various functions, including: an explanation of observed behaviour which contributes to understanding, a basis for predicting future behaviour, a common language, pinpointed direction for further progress, a basis for devising tools and a condensed source for teaching.

Some of the extant literature posits that there is no explicit theory of project management (see for example, Shenhar, 1998; Turner, 1999). Others (including Morris, 1994; Maylor, 2001) point to a growing dissatisfaction with the ability of project management methods and theories to deliver on their promises as a justification for significant re-examination of the dominant doctrines in project management (Cicmil and Hodgson, 2006).

Koskela and Howell (2002) lament the lack of underlying theory in project management, which makes it almost impossible to gain access to the deficient assumptions or to argue with the advocates of the status quo. While agitating for a paradigm change, they note that practitioners continue to observe the short-comings of the approach, blaming the deficient and implicit theoretical foundation for the crisis in the discipline of project management. In their view, the mounting evidence will ultimately result in a paradigmatic transformation that will enable theory and practice to develop concurrently, supporting a continuous dialogue between researchers and practitioners.

Further evidence for a paradigm shift often accumulates as a result of failures and mismatches. Williams (2005) notes the commonality of failing projects in many sectors, identifying a dissonance with the underlying assumptions of the current project management discourse. He invokes Morris's (1994) observation that project management is a 'systems management practice', which 'in many respects is still stuck in a 1960s time warp'. Koskela and Howell (2002) assert that the underlying theory of project management is obsolete. The knowledge promul-gated by the professional associations 'is presented as a set of normative procedures which appear to be self-evidently correct' (Williams, 2005). However, it is com-monly observed that many projects fail in various ways, with Morris and Hough (1987) identifying a fundamentally poor track record of project failure, especi-ally for the larger and more difficult ones. Flyvbjerg et al. (2003) similarly report on major transportation infrastructure projects averaging 90 per cent project over-spend.

Mounting empirical evidence appears to suggest that accepting received project management wisdom, methods and approaches does not appear to either guarantee success or eliminate failure. Koskela and Howell (2002) even suggest that 'in [. . .] big, complex and speedy projects, traditional project management is simply counterproductive; it creates self-inflicted problems that seriously undermine performance'.

Yet it is plausible that in the project world we have failed to evolve our construc-tions and expectations. The Rethinking Project Management Network observed that the bodies of knowledge were initially formulated, and have been subsequently maintained, largely in terms of the certification programmes. Ironically, despite the enormous changes in development in the discipline, the bodies of knowledge appear to have maintained their basic structure (Morris et al., 2006):

> It was Keynes who suggested that people who described themselves as practical men, proud to be uncontaminated by any kind of theory, always turned out to be the intellectual prisoners of the theoreticians of yesteryear.
> (Winter et al., 2006)

Definitions are often constrained by earlier agreed interpretations. Hodgson (2002) points out that claims of the universal and political neutrality of the project management toolkit and approaches lead to an imposed ontology and specific ways of thinking in companies. This implies that normative prescription can be adopted and copied –ultimately, becoming part of a new project reality against which projects are initiated and judged. Questioning the worthiness of the tools and measures, their origin and implications enables an exploration of the epistemological relevance of underlying knowledge and insights.

Pollack (2007) maintains that the theoretical basis of project management is predominantly implicit. Progress in the field would rely on the explicit identification of the underpinning theory in order that assumptions which underline practice can be identified and examined. Smyth and Morris (2007) questioned the epistemological emphasis of knowledge, given the absence of an integrated and unified theory of project management. Academic knowledge is normally developed through detailed elaboration of the epistemological and paradigmatic bases for viewing phenomena. However, project management practice has evolved an eclectic collection of concepts and perspectives.

Lechler and Byrne (2010) indicate that a different perspective is needed to better understand the limitations of project management. Steele (2003, p. 4) points out that: 'radical improvement of project performance is impossible as long as projects are approached in the same way as they have been in the past [. . .] (as current approaches) do not solve the systemic and structural problems that plague projects'. Radical improvement in our understanding thus depends on the ability to reconceive and re-conceptualise project situations in new and meaningful ways.

Discovering our own theories

Many practitioners talk about a mismatch between project management theory and practice. In an ideal world the two are intertwined so that practice is the source of theory, and theory leads to improved practice (Dalcher, 2016). Drawing on experience thus becomes the source for generating the new knowledge required to comprehend the experiences and find their meaning. Continuing to explore and discover enables one to make sense of the environment and function effectively when dealing with unfamiliar contexts and problems.

Knowledge needs to be discovered and utilised in context. Creating our own route in our own work context will enable us to develop our personal theory of problem solving in practice, thus making sense of our deliberations and discoveries.

The prevailing paradigm, or the lens we use for making sense of the world, colours what we can see, so the mismatch can be quite critical. On an individual level, the failure of that dialogue is the failure to connect the received wisdom of accepted theory with the results that we encounter in an increasingly unpredictable and unfamiliar context.

To overcome some of the mismatches, project practitioners increasingly borrow from other disciplines, including change management, business analysis, organisational behaviour, strategic management, value engineering, systems thinking and complexity. This book offers a glimpse into some of the more promising ideas, models and new ways of thinking that have been successfully applied within the context of project practice.

Advances in project management

The individual chapters build on articles that have been selected to feature in the 'Advances in Project Management' series published in the *PM World Journal*. The main purpose of the series is to make the ideas and principles of the knowledge and skills required to manage projects more accessible. *Advances in Project Management* was introduced in order to improve understanding and project capability further up the organisation, amongst strategy and senior decision makers and amongst professional project and programme managers. Our ambition has been to provide project sponsors, project management leaders, practitioners, scholars and researchers with thought-provoking, cutting-edge information that combines conceptual insights with interdisciplinary rigour and practical relevance, thus offering new insights and understanding of key areas and approaches.

In order to identify the potential authors, a wide range of books and resources have been consulted. Contributions were selected by the editor on the basis of their individual merit, usefulness and applicability. The chapters offered here feature many leading practitioners, researchers and leaders and highlight concepts, ideas and tools that will be of benefit to practising project managers.

To this end, the individual chapters aim to:

1 share and embrace new ways of thinking around the challenges faced by project and programme managers;
2 identify and focus on *key* aspects of project, programme and portfolio management;
3 offer practical case examples of how new applications have been tackled in a variety of industries;

4   provide access to appropriate new models in these areas, as they emerge from either academic research or practical application.

In other words, the book aims to provide those people and organisations who are involved with the development of project management with the kind of structured information that will inform their thinking and practice and improve their decisions. In effect, it is new food for thought, intended to invigorate and stimulate the journey of discovery.

Geography and scope

> Knowledge is a treasure, but practice is the key to it.
>
> Laozi

Project management is practised in many different sectors and environments. Such different perspectives allow for the emergence of alternative ideas and ways of thinking. Many of the new ideas develop in different sectors and it is important to find a shared platform to present and highlight the impacts of such innovations and their potential for invigorating current thinking and engendering new insights. This publication offers such a shared environment, which will be of use to practitioners regardless of where they are based and whatever the geography of the projects that they are running.

The book offers a rich diversity of ideas, lessons and insights that are ready to be shared and adopted. The topics emphasise key areas required to improve the delivery of projects and programmes in a wide range of environments and contexts. The experts and authors come from a variety of backgrounds and bring organisational, psychological, sociological or other influences which they can share. Others are experts in coaching, ethics, benchmarking, improvement, marketing, leadership development, strategy, governance and transformational change. The value of the publication is in integrating the multitude of insights and perspectives and offering the opportunity to engage with a rich diversity of approaches and perspectives.

The management of projects offers an exciting space for sharing, collaboration and exploration. The ambition, scale and scope of many of the new endeavours are breath-taking. But an injection of new insights and approaches is desperately needed. Many of our authors are able to offer exciting new approaches for getting there. Together we can continue to develop and grow by embracing new skills and perspectives and improving the state of practice. We encourage readers who would like to share their insights and ideas with the wider community to get in touch with the editor. We look forward to continuing the dialogue about success in projects and extending the boundaries of project and programme management.

Darren Dalcher
London, UK

References

Cicmil, S. & Hodgson, D. (2006). New possibilities for project management theory: A critical engagement. *Project Management Journal, 37*(3), 111–122.

Dalcher, D. (2014). Beyond knowledge: Growing capability for an uncertain future. *Cutter IT Journal, 27*(3), 6–11.

Dalcher, D. (2016). Rethinking project practice: Emerging insights from a series of books for practitioners. *International Journal of Managing Projects in Business, 9*(4), 798–821.

Flyvbjerg, B., Bruzelius, N. & Rothengatter, W. (2003). *Megaprojects and risk: An anatomy of ambition*. Cambridge: Cambridge University Press.

Hodgson, D. (2002). Disciplining the professional: The case of project management. *Journal of Management Studies, 39*(6), 803–821.

Kolb, D. A. (2014). *Experiential learning: Experience as the source of learning and development*. Upper Saddle River, NJ: FT Press.

Koskela, L. & Howell, G. (2002). The underlying theory of project management is obsolete. In De. Slevin, D. Cleland &J. Pinto (Eds), *Proceedings of the PMI Research Conference* (pp. 293–302). Newton Square, PA: Project Management Institute.

Lechler, T. & Byrne, J. C. (2010). *The mindset for creating project value*. Newton Square, PA: Project Management Institute.

Maylor, H. (2001). Beyond the Gantt chart: Project management moving on. *European Management Journal, 19*(1), 92–100.

Morris, P. and Hough, G. (1987). *The anatomy of major projects: A study of the reality of project management*. New York: Wiley.

Morris, P. W. (1994). *The management of projects*. London: Thomas Telford.

Morris, P. W. G., Crawford, L., Hodgson, D., Shepherd, M. M. & Thomas, J. (2006). Exploring the role of formal bodies of knowledge in defining a profession – the case of project management. *International Journal of Project Management, 24*(8), 710–721.

Pollack, J. (2007). The changing paradigms of project management. *International Journal of Project Management, 25*(3), 266–274.

Shenhar, A. (1998). From theory to practice: Toward a typology of project management styles. *IEEE Transactions on Engineering Management, 45*(1), 33–48.

Sibeon, R. (1991). The construction of a contemporary sociology of social work. In M. Davies (Ed.), *The Sociology of Social Work* (pp. 17–67). Routledge, London.

Smyth, H. J. and Morris, P. W. (2007). An epistemological evaluation of research into projects and their management: methodological issues. *International Journal of Project Management, 25*(4), 423–436.

Steele, M. D. (2003). Margins count: Systems thinking and cost. *AACE International Transactions, PM.03*: 03.1–03.5.

Turner, J. R. (1999). Project management: A profession based on knowledge or faith? (Editorial). *International Journal of Project Management, 17*(6), 329–330.

Williams, T. (2005). Assessing and moving on from the dominant project management discourse in the light of project overruns. *IEEE Transactions on Engineering Management, 52*(4), 497–508.

Winter, M., Smith, C., Morris, P. & Cicmil, S. (2006). Directions for future research in project management: The main findings of a UK government-funded research network. *International Journal of Project Management, 24*(8), 638–649.

1
Ethics

IT STARTS WITH TRUST: PEOPLE, PERSPECTIVES AND RELATIONSHIPS AS THE BUILDING BLOCKS FOR SUSTAINABLE SUCCESS

Darren Dalcher

Trust plays a crucial part in many facets of life, including politics, business, sport, friendship, love, marriage and, indeed, all human relationships. Trust appears to be a critical precondition for success in most human endeavours involving more than one individual. Trust can typically appear as a social construct or a psychological belief and may often touch on ethical, personal or organisational values.

The Oxford Dictionary defines trust as 'firm belief in the reliability, truth, or ability of someone or something'. The word *trust* does not appear in the index of the main bodies of knowledge, and only receives a passing mention in the 5th edition of the Project Management Institute (PMI) *Guide to the Body of Knowledge* as a key part of the interpersonal skills of effective project managers. Yet, many aspects of project practice, including teamwork, power, delegation, influencing, reporting, stakeholder engagement and even leadership, intimately rely on the establishment and continued preservation of trust between individuals, team members, parties and organisations.

Assessing the crucial role of the concept, American educator, writer and public speaker Stephen R. Covey observed that 'trust is the glue of life. It's the most essential ingredient in effective communication. It's the foundational principle that holds all relationships together' (Covey, 1995, p. 203).

The five paradoxes of trust

The issue of trust evokes deeply held practical as well as philosophical contradictions and paradoxes. Revolutionary Russian communist Vladimir Ilyich Lenin opined that 'trust is good, but control is better'. Former US President Ronald Reagan, who held a rather different perspective on world affairs, subsequently borrowed an often-used Russian proverb that translates as 'trust, but verify' and used it as the basis for international relations and negotiations with the Russians. International relations often uncover perplexing dependencies and relationships as partners and competitors share, reflect, respond and copy strategies. None the less, the issue of trust and our interaction with the concept continues to offer confounding enigmas and quandaries which will be explored through the lens of the five (plus one) paradoxes of trust.

Paradox 1: Knowing and trusting: when does trust begin?

In order to trust someone, you need to know them: however, you cannot know someone without trusting them first.

The implication of this paradox is that trust requires a leap of faith that obliges one side to give the benefit of the doubt to a relatively unknown and 'unproven' person. While partial mitigation can take views and assessments from other interested parties, such as relying on the word of family members, friends, colleagues or former partners, there is still a certain degree of embracing uncertainty through opening up a potential vulnerability to an unknown person or entity.

Paul Zak and his colleagues offer a neurobiological explanation of trust-building focused on the production of brain chemicals which affect behaviour: when someone shows you trust, it results in the release of oxytocin in the brain, triggering an urge to reciprocate. Oxytocin is a neuropeptide that plays a key role in social attachment and affiliation in non-human mammals, and also causes an increase in trust amongst humans – thereby greatly increasing the benefits from social interaction. Ultimately, the response to trust and the reciprocity that it fosters create a perpetual trust-building cycle. None the less, trust still relies on either party initiating the dynamics of unconditional offering of their blind trust, and thereby corroborating that only trust begets trust.

Paradox 2: Balancing potential success and vulnerability

Ambition for greater success exposes enhanced vulnerabilities.

In order to build stronger relationships and achieve through greater partnerships and alliances, one must embrace new and untested opportunities, thereby exposing oneself to potentially fresh vulnerabilities. The confidence of aiming at new targets and delivering innovative achievements is thus tempered by the additional vulnerabilities that emerge from the relationships and the dependencies that underpin and support the dynamics required to make the new achievements materialise.

Arnold Relman, former editor of the *New England Journal of Medicine*, identified a similar tension within science and research. 'It seems paradoxical', he pondered, 'that scientific research, in many ways one of the most questioning and sceptical of human activities, should be dependent on personal trust. But the fact is that without trust, the research enterprise could not function.'

Indeed, human achievement and social development are predicated on such reliance that allows alliance, cooperation, partnership and collaboration to underpin growth and sustain achievement. Ironically, in order to become bigger and stronger, we seem to need to allow ourselves to become more vulnerable: indeed, the stronger we are, the more the vulnerabilities and dependencies that we may be harbouring . . .

Paradox 3: Difficult to build; but easy to destroy

> *Trust takes a significant effort to build over long time; but,*
> *it can be irredeemably destroyed in an instant.*

Effort is not proportional to achievement; instead it depends on the stage of the relationship. Once trust is lost, it is practically impossible to re-establish. It can take very little effort to derail years of established relationship through a minor detail, a divergent viewpoint or a misunderstanding. Put differently, the evidence required to distrust something, even after it had been held in trust for a significant period, appears to be less demanding and less conclusive. A single incident, a minor failure or a minute breach of confidence or trust can set back the most dedicated relationship or partnership and jeopardise future cooperation.

Moreover, such feelings carry over from one incident or domain to other facets of life, impacting on the way partners and collaborators are perceived in other arenas:

> Whoever is careless with the truth in small matters cannot be trusted with important matters.
>
> Albert Einstein

Paradox 4: Me versus us: here comes everybody else

> *Without trusting others we could not function as a society; however, being overly*
> *reliant and trustful could also jeopardise our potential prosperity and relative safety.*

Teamwork and cooperation bring other individuals into the conversation. Success is thus devolved from the individual to the wider group or community that they inhabit. The relationships they form become essential to the continued survival and thriving of the wider community. Such reliance on others opens up new vulnerabilities.

When we build teams, organisations and supply chains we become dependent on all parts of the network or the chain. The failure of one agent in a tightly knit and well-connected supply chain can derail the entire network, as other participants who have lost particular capabilities and connections through the normal functioning of the network are suddenly forced to look for alternative means of completing their network and replacing the missing agent. Following a long partnership, partners may discover that certain skills that have been outsourced to others may have been lost and connections with alternative suppliers or clients may no longer exist. Our communities of trust and cooperation may thus bind us into different structures and arrangements that may make us more vulnerable over time as we increasingly learn to rely on others.

Paradox 5: More trust but less trusting

> As the ambitions of modern society become more demanding, trust is increasingly essential in realising the achievements and targets required to make those ambitions come true; yet, trust in institutions, leaders and even experts, is eroding at an unprecedented rate.

While we need to build more trust in order to achieve increasingly ambitious common goals, we seem to be witnessing a societal retreat from awarding trust to representatives, experts and change agents. An increasingly sceptical public is challenging authority and is increasingly too resentful to put its trust in governments, non-governmental organisations, commercial organisations, news services, educational establishments, polling organisations and dedicated interest groups. People increasingly say they can no longer trust our public services, trains, doctors, scientists, banks, newspapers, politicians and even religious figures.

Such a perceived crisis of trust can have a significant impact on the institutions we have built through trust, potentially destabilising society, democracy, individual freedoms and the support structures and assets we have toiled to create on a shared basis. Unless we can regain the lost trust through greater scrutiny, visibility, accountability and control, we may yet emerge less protected, less involved and less able to respond, thrive and prosper in our wider groups and communities.

The ultimate trust paradox: to trust is to risk

Perhaps the biggest underlying paradox is that to trust, which implies a pining for safety and protection, is to risk, to open up, to become in some ways more exposed, vulnerable and dependent. The quality which enables us to achieve more in groups also makes us more dependent on the wider group and the individuals with whom we interact. Under some extreme conditions, the kryptonite of trust can deprive us of the special powers that come from belonging, sharing and colluding with a wider community, leaving us more exposed and vulnerable to some potential scenarios of accident and exploitation.

Developing different viewpoints

One part of the answer is to develop a moral compass that can account for multiple parties and interests that make up every partnership and collaboration.

British army officer Robert Baden-Powell, who provided the inspiration to the world Scout Movement, asserted that 'trust should be the basis for all our moral training'.

Trust implies a deeper recognition of the parties we interact with. In projects and programmes it necessitates a deeper need to engage with stakeholders, define the expected benefits and work on outlining and supporting the relationships and on recognising, advertising and promoting the expectations of all involved parties.

Following the exploration of the paradoxes, we can develop an alternative description of trust: if we accept the core implication of trust, as a willingness to become vulnerable through deeper interconnectivity, we also recognise that it bears new types of risks. However, the increased vulnerability and interconnectivity require a more intimate understanding of the potential cooperation and its intended impacts and implications.

To account for the behaviour of organisations, partnerships and other collaborative arrangements there is a need to identify mechanisms which are able to address multiple sets of concerns reflected in the reality of organisational or interpersonal life. Douglas Long and Ngaire Hunt's contribution to this chapter offers a fresh perspective to address competing concerns and the multiplicity of perspectives. The chapter is derived from the book *The Ethical Kaleidoscope: Values, Ethics and Corporate Governance* by Douglas Long and Zivit Inbar, published by Routledge. It uses a construct of the ethical kaleidoscope developed in the book and applies it to the context of managing various types and arrangements of projects.

The work of Long and Inbar (2016) attempts to make sense of the multiple perspectives related to governance of all kinds of organisations. The research is informed by the challenges faced by company directors as they grapple with tensions and competing demands to lead organisations through the moral, ethical and operational challenges that are found in modern business environments.

The kaleidoscope offers a multi-lens perspective that can account for multiple views, values and issues, informing decision-making and governance structures by incorporating legal as well as moral considerations. Combining the perspectives of intuition, risks, processes and culture allows for a richer exploration of issues and implications, to encourage the adoption of a wider and better-informed perspective.

Return on trust

Russian playwright and master storyteller, Anton Chekhov, observed that 'you must trust or believe in people or life becomes impossible'. Relying on others is important for all undertakings, and particularly so in modern endeavours which invoke greater uncertainty, multiple participants and conflicting objectives and intentions.

Scottish author and poet George MacDonald noted that 'to be trusted is a greater compliment than being loved'. Trust maintains a key role in human and organisational development. Trust leads to openness, approachability, open collaboration, ultimately enabling the harnessing of new opportunities and the collaborative exploitation of bigger and bolder prospects.

Management professor and author Gary Hamel observed that 'trust is not simply a matter of truthfulness, or even constancy. It is also a matter of amity and goodwill. We trust those who have our best interests at heart, and mistrust those who seem deaf to our concerns'.

The range of concerns requires careful balancing and prioritising amongst ethical, financial, legal and other concerns. Tools such as the ethical kaleidoscope proposed by Long and Inbar empower leaders and managers to construct knowledge from a multitude of lenses, cope with new information, confront discrepancies, update their insights and understanding and develop a refined understanding of the multiplicity of concerns and issues.

High-trust collaborations, where trust is sustained over time, tend to outperform risk-averse organisations and structures. This is often reputed to translate into superior products and execution, improved relationships, engaged participation, informed and sustained collaboration, exceptional service, greater loyalty, high-performing teams, low staff turnover, greater adaptability and organisational agility and a higher rate of innovation. Focusing on trust can also transform relationships and refocus agendas and priorities.

Trust reprised

US leadership expert Warren Bennis reflected that 'Trust is the lubrication that makes it possible for organizations to work.'

Developing an enhanced version of smart trust attuned to the modern challenges of society requires engagement with trust, collaboration, knowledge, insights and risk. Above all it requires recognition of the participants and their challenges and issues, but offers an informed perspective for addressing the increased volatility, uncertainty and ambiguity of modernity.

If to trust is to risk, it has to be the right risks, whilst acknowledging the new vulnerabilities. In an era of increasing uncertainty and upheaval, we would do well to re-establish our acquaintance with trust. Otherwise, we are destined to face the downside of risk and the effects of increased vulnerability, tending towards catastrophic mistrust, relational breakdowns and a withdrawal from collaborative organisational participation. The breakdown of trust may also herald a collapse towards a greater inward focus on the individual in isolation – a stage we have managed to eclipse as a society.

Many of the challenges we face require collaborating and working together at the societal and global levels, extending beyond physical boundaries and imposed constraints and limitations. Our ambitions are unprecedented and demanding and can be overcome only through wider collaboration and mutual trust.

The final warning for lack of action comes from the farewell address to the nation by another US president, in a different era:

> This world of ours . . . must avoid becoming a community of dreadful fear and hate, and be, instead, a proud confederation of mutual trust and respect.
>
> Dwight D. Eisenhower, 17 January 1961

Ultimately, only intelligent and informed trust carries within it the necessary seeds for collaboration, hope and future progress.

References

Covey, S. M. (2006). *The speed of trust: The one thing that changes everything.* London: Simon and Schuster.

Covey, S. R., Merrill, A. R. & Merrill, R. R. (1995). *First things first.* London: Simon and Schuster.

Kosfeld, M., Heinrichs, M., Zak, P. J., Fischbacher, U. & Fehr, E. (2005). Oxytocin increases trust in humans. *Nature, 435*(7042), 673–676.

Long, D. G. & Inbar, Z. (2016). *The ethical kaleidoscope: Values, ethics and corporate governance.* Abingdon: Routledge.

PMI (2015). *Guide to the project management body of knowledge* (5th ed.). Newton Square, PA: Project Management Institute.

Zak, P. J. (2008). The neurobiology of trust. *Scientific American, 298*(6), 88–95.

Zak, P. J. (2017). Trust factor: The science of creating high-performance companies. New York: AMACOM.

Zak, P. J., Kurzban, R. & Matzner, W. T. (2004). The neurobiology of trust. *Annals of the New York Academy of Sciences, 1032*(1), 224–227.

THE PROJECT MANAGER AND THE ETHICAL KALEIDOSCOPE

Douglas Long and Ngaire Hunt

Depending on the role held by a project manager (PM), there appear to be three possible scenarios in which the potential exists for ethics conflict:

- if they are a vendor-based PM:
  - how to implement the project to the benefit of the vendor
  - how to implement the project to the benefit of the customer;
- if they are an organisation-based PM:
  - how to implement the project to the benefit of the organisation
  - how to manage the internal stakeholders' expectations and knowledge requirements (as the PM may be provided with information which is confidential or more detailed than that of other stakeholders or team members)
  - how to manage / involve the vendor PM (if a vendor is involved);
- if they are a contracted PM:
  - how to implement the project to the benefit of the customer
  - how to manage the internal stakeholders' expectations and knowledge requirements (as the PM may be provided with information which is confidential or more detailed than that of other stakeholders or team members)
  - how to manage / involve the vendor PM (if a vendor is involved)
  - how to implement the project to the benefit of themselves and the contracting company (if used).

These can arise because:

- multiple stakeholders will have different, and competing, sets of priorities;
- there may also be a distinction between the customer and other stakeholders;
- there may be tensions between the priorities of the project manager and those of the different groups of stakeholders, and also the clients.

In this chapter we explore the application of the Ethical Kaleidoscope as a tool for assisting project managers to confront and deal ethically with conflicting project-owner demands faced in their work. By utilising the lens nominated in the model we seek to provide support to project managers, no matter whether vendor based, organisation based or contracted.

The Ethical Kaleidoscope is a construct developed by Douglas Long and Zivit Inbar to assist boards of organisations – large or small, public or private, government or non-government, for-profit or not-for-profit – to operate not only in ways that meet legal requirements but also in ways that deal ethically with all affected parties. In their research leading to the book (interviews with the chairs of some 130 organisations in Australia, New Zealand and the USA), Long and Inbar found that the main emphasis at a corporate governance level related primarily to the legality of activities, with any ethical considerations often relegated to a very poor secondary or tertiary position, very often of only cursory concern. The result is that, even when an organisation has a clear and published code of ethics (as was the case for many of those studied), the incidence of organisations behaving badly occurs far too frequently.

Although the model nominates the lens as being intuition, board risks, external risks, internal processes and organisational culture (Figure 1.1), at least one lens is capable of being relabelled if the kaleidoscope is being used by parties other than the board. Applying this model to the role of the project manager, we suggest that the lens through which the project manager considers their ethical obligations should be:

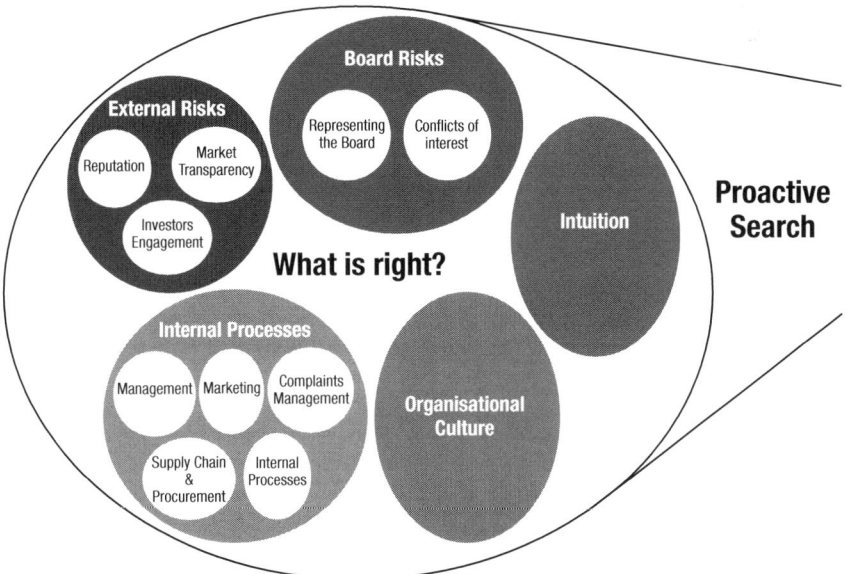

FIGURE 1.1 The Ethical Kaleidoscope

- organisational intuition
- organisational risks
- external risks
- internal processes
- organisational culture.

Organisational intuition

One of the chairs interviewed by Long and Inbar commented that, long before he was able to show that an ethical issue existed and that the board needed to act, he had 'a gut feeling' that something was 'not quite right'. It was this 'gut feeling' that prompted him to further investigations. Other chairs admitted to having similar 'feelings about the ethical correctness of something', yet went on to say that, once they had ascertained the activity was legal, they took no further action.

As a project manager (PM), Ngaire Hunt has sometimes felt that something was 'off' with the progression of the project or that a stakeholder group might be affected (either positively or negatively) by continuing the current course of the project. 'It's at that moment, I as the PM have choices – do I sit by and continue the current course? Do I review the project charter and scope to understand if the project is on the right track or do I raise my "off" feeling to the Project Steering Committee (PSC) to reference that there may be an ethical issue with the current course? In my experience, I have found that reviewing the charter and scope while wearing an ethical lens from the view of the stakeholder group that I am concerned about, enables me to raise any potential ethical risks to the PSC for appropriate course corrections.'

If a person clearly understands and is committed to the ethics of their profession, then a finely tuned values set can often provide an early indicator of potential problems long before any tangible evidence appears. How finely tuned is your values meter? Do you listen to your ethical intuition? If your intuitive concerns are then corroborated by facts, what action do you take?

Organisational risks

Every project has an economic and social impact on the organisation. Sometimes the impact can be so great that project failure could have seriously adverse effects on the organisation's viability; others, of course, may have more of an impact on the project champion's ego than on organisational sustainability, but both economic issues and ego need to be considered.

In July 2016 the Australian Federal Government introduced data-matching software to ascertain the eligibility of people to receive various social benefits. The philosophy behind the project was (and is) sound – to ensure that those people eligible for support receive that to which they are entitled and that the social welfare system is not cheated. However, as the project was rolled out towards the end of 2016 and into 2017 it was clear that, despite the protestations from various

Ministers of the Crown and Departmental Heads, the system had serious ethical and practical flaws and urgent remedial attention was required. Quite clearly, only the needs of the government had been taken into account, with the needs of those affected being written off as of little or no real importance. As at the time of writing it appears as though the egos of politicians and senior public servants are trumping other concerns, with the result that a long-term impact of the refusal to listen to public and media feedback and to correct identified problems may be the non-re-electability of the present government, should it be decided to call an election in the relatively near future.

When considering organisational risks, does the project manager consider not just the short-term future but also the far more complex medium- to long-term impact of the project on both the organisation per se and the project champions? How do you manage this – especially if you have had no involvement in the project-planning phase? At what point in the implementation process do you provide project reports that include cost-benefit analyses broader than simply a question of economics? What do you do when the project owner refuses to listen to (or otherwise ignores) your feedback?

External risks

As already indicated, the reputation of both the organisation and the project champions can be at risk in a project. However, there may also be more direct external risks. For example, when working on a project which potentially impacts the lives of everyday people, one of the risks is that if it is implemented differently at each of the affected sites, the end result may vary according to the success of the project due to the amount of time taken at each of the sites to achieve the desired outcome. How does the project manager ensure that there is consistency of approach and outcomes for each of the sites? Ngaire fondly remembers a case where each site had a dedicated project team which could draw on the knowledge and experience of both the originating project team as well as others that were implementing at the same time. This enabled external risks to be assessed and managed effectively and with a high level of consistency across all sites.

How frequent and effective is your monitoring of external risks? Is the sharing of information full and open, or (all too often because of ego and/or power and control issues) is there a tendency to operate on a strict 'need to know' basis in which some teams are left to second-guess what might have happened elsewhere?

Internal processes

Almost always, projects impact on one or more of the internal processes of an organisation – management, procurement, marketing, service etc. Sometimes, in the planning stage, inadequate attention has been given to the symbiotic relationship necessary between these, especially when implementing a brand new methodology in which, as the methodology develops and is expanded and refined, the steps required to effectively implement also change. All information pertaining to such changes needs to be mapped and explained, with all the pieces of the puzzle being shown in their interconnectivity, to enable the methodology and process to be understood and followed. If this is incomplete, then the associated project teams implementing the new methodology may be unable to ensure that the processes they are following are as they should be now (rather than as they were previously planned) and what they are likely to be as the project moves to future stages.

How compartmentalised are the organisation and the project? Do different areas jealously guard their way of doing things? Can you easily get the information you need? Do you readily share, in a way that others can understand, the information which you have? Do you update 'the big picture' as well as the composite pieces?

Organisational culture

Different organisational cultures necessitate differing approaches. No two cultures are identical (although there may be many similarities) and such differences present a range of ethical issues. Following the (Federal Government) forced merger of three retail electricity suppliers in 2017, it became clear that some 1,500 staff would be surplus to requirements once the transition was completed. This decision was made despite the board knowing that the needs of the owners (the government), the organisation, the employees and customers were different and, in some instances, opposing. In this instance the chair and chief executive were staunch believers in very open communication and ensured that this news was given to every employee. They emphasised that the end result was a given, but that the process towards this result was open to discussion and input from all affected parties. Two years later the project was completed on time, within budget and with no industrial unrest or customer complaints about service. Past employees still speak positively about their previous employer and the way the project was managed. All too often organisations try to keep information sharing to a minimum. How does the project manager handle these two extremes (or anything in between), especially if the rumour mill is actually accurate but the organisation doesn't want the truth to be known? Where is the dividing line between a functional and dysfunctional organisational culture in relation to project implementation? How does the project manager handle any conflict between their own value set and the restrictions imposed by management?

When a young boy, Douglas Long was given a toy that enthralled him. It looked like a short telescope but, rather than only expanding to change focus, it also had a rotating body that, as one moved it, enabled a variety of different patterns to be seen. Only when the full range of colours and patterns had been viewed could the picture again be seen in its entirety. In the intervening time the viewer could see only aspects of the picture, through different colours and different patterns. It was a kaleidoscope.

As a project manager you have an extremely important role to fulfil. All too often the pressures you face can seduce you into maintaining a relatively narrow focus on what is necessary in order to bring the project in on time and within budget. You are, if you like, operating with a telescope that enables both short and long focus as necessary. Sometimes, however, you also need a kaleidoscope – a visual tool for maintaining the same focus but viewing the picture through a range of different colours and patterns. The Ethical Kaleidoscope is designed to help you do just that: never lose sight of the big picture, but also use the kaleisdoscope to maximise the probability that you are considering the broadest possible range of complexities. A tightrope walker needs to proceed along the length of the rope while maintaining balance amid a variety of external forces. Project managers need many tightrope-walker skills!

In summary, the role of project management is both essential and complex. Ethical issues are often hidden and very hard to read. Using the Ethical Kaleidoscope can help project managers to ensure that they consider and confront the complexity of ethical considerations necessary to deliver a performance that not only meets organisational requirements but also is in full accord with the profession's own code of ethics.

2

People

WHAT HAS TAYLOR EVER DONE FOR US? SCIENTIFIC AND HUMANE MANAGEMENT RECONSIDERED

Darren Dalcher

Pioneers pave the path for those who follow by shaping the discipline and defining the terrain. They also play a crucial role in surfacing and enshrining basic assumptions that permeate thinking and logic around the emerging discipline. As a leading pioneer in the development of management thinking, Taylor's influence on the discipline of project management merits exploration and analysis in the context of the wider philosophy of management.

Fredrick Winslow Taylor (1856–1915) is considered a principal innovator in industrial engineering, especially in relation to improving efficiency and utilising time and motion studies. He is particularly renowned for establishing the *principles of scientific management*, through the publication of a monograph of that title in 1911.

Taylor was born into a wealthy Quaker family from Philadelphia, yet started his professional life on the factory floor as an apprentice pattern-maker. He became a chief engineer at Midvale Steel Works, before moving to the Bethlehem Steel Company, where he pioneered time and motion studies, analysing how each specific job could be done more efficiently. He was often seen walking around the factory floor with a stopwatch and note-pad, breaking down manual tasks into a series of components that could be measured (Hindle, 2008, p. 309). According to Drucker (1974, p. 181), Taylor was 'the first man in history who did not take work for granted, but looked at it and studied it'. Moreover, Drucker also maintained that, between them, Charles Darwin, Henry Ford and Taylor were the makers of the modern world.

Taylor has been instrumental in the development of modern management. *The Principles of Scientific Management* was the first business book bestseller. The text has inspired administrators and efficiency aficionados to adopt productivity-enhancing and waste-reducing procedures and measures. The influence of the book has endured for over a century and the many translations have been known to inspire the writing of Henri Fayol in France; the development of the movement for scientific management in the UK headed by Major Lyndall Urwick, who would later become Britain's first professional management consultant; the efficiency and improvement schemes of Italy's Mussolini; and the target setting advocated by Lenin for Soviet workers. While failure to meet explicit production targets may have directed Soviet workers to the gulag (Hindle, 2008, p. 310), the principles of scientific management remain at the core of modern management thinking, underpinning a great deal of theory and concepts in administrative studies, work design, industrial-era organisation and decision theory.

A 1997 *Fortune* article noted that: 'Taylor's influence is omnipresent. It's his ideas that determine how many burgers McDonald's expects its flippers to flip or how many callers the phone company expects its operators to assist' (Farnham, 1997).

What's the big idea?

According to the *Economist Guide to Management Ideas and Gurus*, scientific management was the first big management idea to reach a mass audience as it swept through corporate America in the early years of the twentieth century before spreading to continental Europe and the rest of the world. Moreover, the Guide also claims that a significant proportion of subsequent management thinking has been either a reaction to scientific thinking or a development of it (Hindle, 2008, p. 159).

The label 'scientific management' is borrowed from the work of US lawyer and judge Louis Dembitz Brandeis, who described the need to coordinate enterprise to everyone's benefit. Likewise, Taylor was a strong believer in increasing the total benefits and welfare of all participants.

> The principal object of management should be to secure the maximum prosperity for the employer coupled with the maximum prosperity for each employee.
>
> (Taylor, 1911, p. 9)

The imperative to improve efficiency quotes US President Theodore Roosevelt's reflection that 'The conservation of our national resources is only preliminary to the larger question of national efficiency'.

Scientific management was thus positioned to stem national inefficiency, through the proposed universal remedy of systematic management. The explicit purpose of *Scientific Management* was therefore:

> To prove that the best management is a true science, resting upon clearly defined laws, rules, and principles, as a foundation. And further to show that the fundamental principles of scientific management are applicable to all kinds of human activities, from our simplest individual acts to the work of our great

corporations, which call for the most elaborate cooperation. And, briefly, through a series of illustrations, to convince the reader that whenever these principles are correctly applied, results must follow which are truly astounding.

(Taylor, 1911, p. 9)

Scientific management

Scientific management boils down to five simple principles (Morgan, 1997, p. 23).

1 Shift all responsibility for the organisation of the work from the worker to the manager.
2 Use scientific methods to determine the most efficient methods for completing the work (while specifying the precise way in which the work is to be done).
3 Select the best person to perform the 'designed' job.
4 Train the worker to do the work efficiently.
5 Monitor worker performance to ensure the appropriate method is followed and that the appropriate results are achieved.

The principles imply total visibility, strict accountability and absolute control. Indeed, according to Taylor (1903), the art of management had been defined 'As knowing exactly what you want men to do, and then seeing that they do it in the best and cheapest way.'

The origins of scientific management lay in Taylor's observations of his fellow workers, recognising that they had no incentive to work harder or go faster, as ultimately it was in their interest to keep their employers ignorant of how fast work can be done. Noting that the workers had a clear advantage in knowing how fast they could actually work, Taylor measured and examined all aspects of work to derive an understanding of what each task entailed, thereby engaging in an organised 'pursuit of more' (Crainer, 2000, p. 9).

Measuring each and every task enabled organisations to estimate and predict the duration of jobs involving multiple tasks. Work could thus be scheduled, monitored and controlled using the new knowledge regarding individual tasks and their expected durations. Moreover, it enabled specific processes to be re-engineered and improved for efficiency purposes.

Taylor's crucial contribution was to invent management as science through the application of rigour and discipline that comes from observation and measurement (Crainer, 2000, p. 11). Scientific management established the manager as a supervisor engaged in measurement, laying the foundation of the philosophy that 'what gets measured, gets done'. In the process, it created a new middle layer of management, a new stratum concerned with observation and measurement of efficiency. Crainer notes the ironic twist that the man most dedicated to efficiency thus created one of the most significant barriers to business efficiency and decision making (ibid.).

Separating thinking from doing

After Taylor was promoted from operator to 'gang boss' in the machine shop at Midvale, the workers asked him not to interfere with the allocations of work. His answer was that, as an operator, he did not break a single rate set by the group but that, as a supervisor, he intended to get more work out of them (Savage, 1996, p. 171).

> In the past the man has been first; in the future the system must be first.
>
> (Taylor, 1911, p. 7)

Taylor's first-hand experience on the factory floor convinced him that it was necessary to gain control of the production process. In order to improve efficiency, he believed that managers were required to do all the thinking related to the planning and design of work, leaving workers with the task of implementation. Jobs were often simplified to ensure that workers would be cheap, easy to train and easily replaceable. Through the singular and all-consuming focus on efficiency Taylor turned men into machines: a non-personal, static and obedient resource used for their muscle power.

> In our scheme, we do not ask the initiative of our men. We do not want any initiative. All we want of them is to obey the orders we give them, do what we say, and do it quick.
>
> (Taylor, 1911, p. 11).

The purpose of collecting scientific data was to facilitate the separation between planning and doing:

> Thus all of the planning which under the old system was done by the workman, as a result of his personal experience, must by necessity under the new system be done by the management in accordance with the laws of science . . . It is also clear that in most cases one type of man is needed to plan ahead and an entirely different type to execute the work.
>
> (Ibid., p. 38)

The basic unit of work for both measurement and allocation was the 'task', which became the single unit of scientific management. Taylor's idea was that the planning office would provide comprehensive, written-up instructions specifying what was to be done, how it was to be done and how long it would take to complete the tasks. Workers would simply be tasked with executing the instructions.

> This separation of thinkers from doers was the apogee of specialization: Planning was to be distinct from execution. Brain distinct from brawn, head from hand, white collar from blue collar.
>
> (Reich, 1983, p. 63)

The principle of separating the planning and design from execution, and the intended desire of freeing the workers from the need to think flow naturally from the desire to simplify tasks, improve efficiency and throughput, reduce waste and increase monitoring and control. They are also responsible for many of the dysfunctional aspects of life cycles and work schemes that we still employ nowadays. Note, for example, the growing interest in agile development, which involves stakeholders in the requirements and design activities through rapid iterative cycles of learning and development, thereby overcoming the artificial separation imposed on the cycle of work for managerial and efficiency reasons. Likewise the assumptions that execution cannot proceed until the full and exact details of what needs to be done have been completed also features in some environments and life-cycle configurations that persist in maintaining a purely sequential approach rather than allowing for progressive or iterative elaboration of detail. Prototyping and agile approaches re-establish the value of intertwined planning and development, requirements and design, allowing products, knowledge and expectations to evolve and adapt based on emerging needs, improved insights and continuing engagement.

Removing expertise and knowledge

One side-effect of Taylor's approach was the replacement of skilled craftspeople with unskilled workers trained only to do specific tasks in prescribed ways.

> In the words of historian Steven Diner, Taylorism robbed workers of 'all matters of judgements about their jobs: What tools to use, in what order tasks should be performed, how many pounds they should lift at one time, how fast they should work, when they should rest – in short, every aspect of control over work.'
>
> (Cherny, 2002, p. 162)

As part of the apparent deskilling, workers thus lost valuable expertise, knowledge and crucial judgement and decision-making skills that could have been shared with other professionals. The resulting inability to think, adapt and respond to change and deviation also means that specialist knowledge and insights and the ability to make professional judgements were removed from the professional workforce and transferred to the new management cadres, further deskilling future generations while degrading, and even eliminating, craftsmanship, professionalism and ethics from the front line of workers.

Taylor's biographer Robert Kanigel (2005, p. 498) observed that 'after Ford and Taylor got through with them, most jobs needed less of everything – less brains, less muscle, less independence'.

Ironically, it would seem that the rigid and inflexible 'pursuit of more' that provided the impetus for scientific management had ultimately resulted in securing less all around . . .

Implications of scientific management

Taylorism confers power to those in control: the wide adoption of scientific management in capitalist settings, as well as in many autocratic and socialist regimes, signifies that it is as much a tool for securing general control over the workplace as it is a means of generating profit (Morgan, 1997; Hanlon, 2015).

Scientific management was a product of its time: as people moved from agriculture to the cities and engaged in industrial tasks, its chief concern was with adding a lens that could focus on management, improvement and control, thereby enabling an improved ability to plan, estimate and measure employees' combined work.

On the positive side, Taylor's input to scientific management offered a number of benefits and longer-term impacts:

- great efficiency of performance
- making management a relevant discipline and study area
- emergence of time studies
- a new focus on tasks
- an emphasis on measurement, and later on quality management.

Yet, the shift towards a machine way of thinking about people in the workplace has been responsible for other impacts, raising new concerns, criticisms and challenges, including:

- life never as controlled and predictable as Taylor envisaged
- difficulty in adapting to changing circumstances
- context-specific measurement under stable conditions, offering limited universal credibility
- inhumane character of the approach: lack of attention to employees and their needs
- treating employees as robots/machines
- ignoring moral and ethical aspects
- promise of improved efficiency at societal level, never materialised
- encouragement of uniformity of thinking
- potential to result in mindless and unquestioning bureaucracy
- potential to result in unanticipated and undesirable consequences
- stifling innovation
- stripping the organisation of flexibility and resilience
- ignoring new problems (as there are no mechanisms for addressing them)
- paralysis, inaction or excessive meetings to deal with unexpected events
- raising of segmentation, silos and internal barriers
- consequently, a general inability to solve problems in proper context
- possibility of information being distorted
- organisational passivity to change
- apathy, carelessness and lack of pride

- discouraging initiative
- sub-optimisation instead of global excellence
- limiting rather than building on individual strengths, potential or capabilities
- employees unable to develop or grow
- not suited to modern times
- unnatural separation between planning and doing
- deskilling workers.

> Fredrick Taylor's 'Scientific Management', well adapted to the simple industrial companies of the early century, has been stretched to the limits of its applicability. We now struggle with the costly and discouraging side effects of ... 'production first, people second': declining productivity, dissatisfaction with work, hatred and hostility as the basis of a general union-management deadlock, loss of pride in workmanship and the near extinction of workers' organisational pride.
>
> (Butteress & Albrecht, 1979)

What about the people involved?

Many organisational psychologists despair of the Taylor's legacy. In his endeavour to maximise manual efficiency, Taylor abandoned the nuances and strengths of human nature and capability, displaying psychological illiteracy. Indeed, a key criticism of Taylor's approach was that he treated people as machines.

> We never had any use for Taylor or any of the efficiency or scientific management crowd. They never realized that human toil was the last thing in the world you had to be efficient about.
>
> (Scott, 1965)

A key omission from Taylor's work was interest in human relations and the impact of change and tinkering in the workplace on individuals, their health, dedication, motivation, performance, confidence, capability, decision-making skills, innovation and willingness to support the organisation.

One of the early critics of Taylor's work, often credited with initiating the human factors or human relations movement, is Lillian Gilbreth, who was interested in exploring the psychological element within management in order to complement and augment the scientific management perspective. Her book, *The Psychology of Management: The Function of the Mind in Determining, Teaching and Installing Methods of Least Waste*, was published in 1914. The work emerged from her doctoral dissertation at the University of California. When the university refused to grant Gilbreth the degree, due to her failure to complete the residency requirements, she published her research in a series of articles in *Industrial Engineering and Engineering Digest*, before releasing the full manuscript in 1914.

Throughout the book, Gilbreth contends that scientific management recognises the individual not only as an economic unit of production but also as a personality. Management must therefore encompass the human element, thereby rising beyond Taylorism to address the fuller scope of managing. The book itself emphasises knowledge of the individual, the theory of groups, theory of communication and the rational basis for decision making. Its contribution has been essential in positioning psychology in the context of management and emphasising its role and value over a century ago, at a time when Taylor was still promoting the concept of the employee as a machine. Gilbreth's book has been singled out by scholars as culturally important and is recognised as part of the knowledge base of civilisation, indicating its role as an influential founding text. Lillian and her husband, Frank Gilbreth, are credited as bringing together two of the main streams of management thinking. Although their work has become less popular nowadays, Lillian Gilbreth is still recognised as the 'first lady of management' (Hindle, 2008, p. 244).

From efficient to effective management

Taylor's focus featured an acknowledged national need and a lasting obsession with improving efficiency. By concentrating on efficiency he had managed to discount and ignore human factors and needs, addressing tasks and their execution without considering the operator and their impact. Reducing humans to machines has enabled management to address efficiency concerns and make advances in the areas of time and motion, work allocation, quality assurance, process re-engineering and process improvement. Yet, it is also worth noting that not all the changes and improvements proposed by Taylor were accepted; indeed, following resistance by the workers, Taylor himself was fired in 1901, bringing an end to his practical experiments.

Gilbreth made important advances by progressing the search for efficiency to bring the human subjects and participants into consideration. Other advances around human relations, human activity systems, ergonomics, human-centred design and human interaction followed over time. Yet, some of the classical ideas of 'Taylorism' still persist within management thinking and organisation. Psychology has a lot to contribute to management in general, and more specifically to the management of projects. Projects are done in groups; they require team members to communicate, empathise, comprehend, influence and engage. Moreover, there is a crucial need to understand what motivates individuals to improve performance within teams, and to encourage the adoption of proposed change. Delivering successful projects requires an understanding of people and psychology.

The chapter by Fred Voskoboynikov significantly advances that agenda by encouraging a deeper consideration of the psychological aspects of management, highlighting the role of the human element in managing. The chapter draws upon his book *The Psychology of Effective Management: Strategies for Relationship Building*, published by Routledge. Throughout this work, Voskoboynikov distils the practical implications of good management practice that are centred on human performance and achievement.

Voskoboynikov acknowledges the dramatic changes in human work which, in contradiction of Taylor's view, increasingly require greater reliance on human intelligence, knowledge and insights. In order to address such a wider agenda, new fields such as work physiology and occupational psychology are needed to integrate human capabilities and improve performance. Excelling and enhancing performance emerges from an understanding of the participants and their strengths and capabilities. The implication is that, in order to improve performance and deliver, organisations need to employ conductors who are able to bring different skills and expertise together, rather than efficiency experts and drill sergeants who endeavour to optimise individual tasks and minutiae.

The importance of the work is in shifting the conversation from an obsession with small-scale yet continuous improvement of the repetitive, towards a deeper understanding of the need to combine a range of skills and capabilities and adapt and adjust on the basis of the characteristics of the situations we encounter. Voskoboynikov (2017) is therefore able to progress the discussion from one concerned with mechanistic *efficiency* of operations and reduction of waste, towards one that addresses the challenges of modern life by embracing and acknowledging the role of *effectiveness*, and fitness-for-purpose management. The richness of working with people can therefore be used to excel, improve and grow performance through the use of human capabilities, factors and relationships.

Returning to Taylor and efficiency

Taylor's legacy is a mixed bag of insights and findings. His obsession with efficiency coloured his interests and perspective: whilst still at college, he succeeded in changing the official rules of baseball by proving that over-arm bowling was more efficient than under-arm bowling. Alas, other efficiency work proving that tennis rackets shaped as spoons and Y-shaped golf putters are more efficient did not ultimately alter those respective sports.

The obsession with a single factor, such as efficiency, can often obscure other relevant perspectives and stifle further development. While Taylor was a pioneering leader and guide in a time of much uncertainty, his approach was limited, as it overlooked uncertainty and ignored the role of human beings. Legislating for machines does not abolish human tendencies and concerns. The addition of psychology and human-factor thinking to the repertoire of the management practitioner is an important and necessary augmentation of perspective.

Ultimately, Taylor was a complex and controversial figure, whom Morgan (1997, p. 385) refers to as a man with an obsessive vision backed by a determination to implement it at all costs.

American engineer Henry Laurence Gantt similarly observed that Taylor was 'endowed naturally with untiring energy and a wonderfully analytical mind, he concentrated all the power of that combination on the problem of determining the facts he needed.'

Efficiency, or 'doing things right', is crucial, but only as long as we also ensure that we continue to be effective by 'doing the right things' – because ultimately there is nothing worse and more wasteful than doing the wrong things but with an extreme, and forever improving, efficiency.

References

Butteress, M. & Albrecht, K. (1979). *New management tools*. Englewood, NJ: Prentice-Hall.

Cherny, A. (2002). *The next deal: The choice revolution and the new responsibility*. New York: Basic Books.

Crainer, S. (2000). *The management century: A critical review of 20th century thought and practice*. San Francisco: Jossey-Bass.

Drucker, P. F. (1974). *Management: Tasks, responsibilities, practices*. New York: Harper Collins.

Farnham, A. (1997, 21 July). The man who changed forever. *Fortune*, p. 14.

Gilbreth, L. M. (1914). *The psychology of management: The function of the mind in determining, teaching and installing methods of least waste*. New York: Sturgis and Walton.

Hanlon, G. (2015). *The dark side of management: A secret history of management theory*. Abingdon: Routledge.

Hindle, T. (2008). *Guide to management ideas and gurus*. London: The Economist.

Kanigel, R. (2005). *The one best way: Frederick Winslow Taylor and the enigma of efficiency*. Waltham: MIT Press Books.

Morgan, G. (1997). *Images of organization* (2nd ed.). Thousand Oaks, CA: Sage.

Reich, R. B. (1983). *The next American frontier: A provocative program for economic renewal*. New York: Penguin Books.

Savage, C. M. (1996). *5th generation management: On creating through virtual enterprising, dynamic teaming and knowledge networking*. Newton, MA: Butterworth-Heinemann.

Scott, H. (1965). History and Purpose of Technocracy. *Northwest Technocrat* (July), 7–8.

Taylor, F. W. (1903). Shop management; a paper read before the American society of mechanical engineers. *Transactions of the American Society of Mechanical Engineers, 24*, 1337–1480.

Taylor, F. W. (1911). *The principles of scientific management*. New York: Harper & Brothers.

Taylor, F. W. (1919). *Two papers on scientific management: A piece-rate system and notes on belting*. London: George Routledge.

Urwick, L. F. & Brech, E. F. L. (1945). *The making of scientific management* (Vol. 2). London: Management Publications Trust.

Voskoboynikov, F. (2017). *The psychology of effective management: Strategies for relationship building*. New York: Routledge.

ON THE PSYCHOLOGICAL ASPECT OF MANAGEMENT

Fred Voskoboynikov

Introduction

Most of the attention in any organisation is directed towards achieving financial goals, i.e. towards profitability. This is vital for the organisation and well understood. However, particularly for this reason, people's interests are not often on the priority list in organisations' affairs. When that is the case, sooner or later the approach will backfire and prevent the organisation from functioning successfully in the long run. Hence, directing all possible efforts toward creating a positive psychological environment in the workplace is of a significant importance. To create such an environment without a basic knowledge of psychology does not seem possible. To know people's individual characteristics, their ability to work in a group environment as well as their values, goals and desires, is just as necessary for managers as to possess technical knowledge in their chosen field of activity. People are filled with thoughts and ideas, and they want to experience satisfaction from their implementation. To achieve the desired objectives and maintain satisfaction in the workplace, one must be prepared to think of people in human terms (Voskoboynikov, 2017).

Regardless of the type of organisation and the field of activity, general managerial functions are similar. In fact, management functions are considered to be universal. Managers plan and organise, coordinate and control, make decisions and handle physical, informational and financial resources, create and communicate, motivate and reward, and so on. However, all of this comes down to managing people. A bank manager does not manage safes and accounts, a construction manager does not manage construction equipment and materials, a ship captain does not hold the steering wheel himself but gets to the desired destination by managing the ship's crew.

In this brief chapter, we will consider some important factors of a psychological nature which should be taken into account in managers' work with people.

Individual approach

To take an individual–focused approach in management is perhaps the most crucial role of the manager. To see employees as individuals and recognise their abilities and desires helps to bring out the best in them. Each person has a unique personality; some people are good at one thing, while others are good in something else. Hence, the golden rule in dealing with people is not try to change people but, rather, to build on what they are and compensate for what they are not. To give a person the wrong role is akin to asking him to be what he is not. When one is pressed to be what he is not, he does not feel good and does not perform as effectively. But when placed in his comfort zone, where he feels 'in his shoes', everything changes – he feels good, his productivity increases and all the rest that comes with it. Then people around him are amazed about the changes in him. But he has not changed, he simply has become himself. Morris Viteles, who is considered to be one of the fathers of industrial psychology and an enthusiast of putting the human element into the practice of management, wrote: 'It is important that a man be kept out of a job for which he is not fitted. It is even more important that he be placed in a job where he can be efficient and happy' (as cited in Wallace, 1996). Such an approach should be a sort of guiding star for managers in their work with people.

The compatibility factor

The group is not the arithmetical sum of separate individuals, and the result of group performance is not always the positive sum of the results of individual performances by the members. Just as two dozen clear fragments of glass stacked one on top of another provide a rich blue colour, or a combination of copper and tin results an alloy whose hardness resides in neither of them, similarly, people in a group act and behave in a new capacity, as components of the system 'individual – other individuals'. Representatives of various professions and other kinds of activity such as polar explorers, mountain climbers, commanders of aircraft and ships' crews, coaches of athletic teams and many others experience in real life that not all people are equally fit for complex teamwork. That is, speaking in the language of psychology, 'two plus two is not always four'.

According to Aristotle the whole is greater than the sum of its parts. No disrespect to Aristotle, but the sum of the parts does not automatically become a 'greater whole' just because of the presence of the required parts. This suggests that for the effective execution of tasks in a group environment not only the presence of needed specialists and their technical skills should be taken into account, but also the degree of compatibility between them. Depending on the degree of compatibility, the result of group performance may either be equal to the sum of the results of individual performances, or greater or less than that sum. Examples of incompatibility can be seen in a work crew where there is a significant difference in workers' skills, or an athletic team formed of athletes of different skill levels. This kind of incompatibility is called *physiological*. In these examples such physical parameters such as height, physical strength, motor skills etc. are described. To note such differences in people is not that difficult and it's unlikely that anyone would instruct people with such differences to perform a task where these differences present a hindrance.

People always experience certain flow of feelings toward others within the group. These feelings are based on differences of a psychological nature, such as temperament, character, social orientation, habits, amateur interests, religious and ethnic peculiarities and others. They may be positive or negative, or neutral; they can be weak or strong in intensity; they can be mutual or non-mutual and therefore conflicting. These differences are not always obvious and apparent. However, differences of this kind quite often have a decisive impact on compatibility and, in turn, on the successful implementation of the group task. The incompatibility due to the described differences is called *psychological*. The presence of psychological incompatibility is a major obstacle for effective group performance.

Psychological incompatibility has a negative influence not only on group performance but also on human health. Unfriendly, uptight relationships between group members in the working environment bring up negative emotions. In mass professions where there are no expressed extreme conditions people can perform productively under the influence of negative emotions for a fairly long time. However, it's important to understand that all of this is at the expense of unnecessary stress, that is accepted temporarily, in the knowledge that an end point will be reached. Many can recall a depressing mental state due to incompatibility with colleagues or bosses at a current or previous job. Working in a background environment of negative emotions for a long period of time may cause pathological developments in the central nervous system, which can lead to various diseases of a neurotic type. People become irritable, experience headaches, insomnia, blood pressure disorders, dysfunction of the gastrointestinal tract and other health problems. Typical medical approaches to the treatment of such conditions do not always have positive results. There are statistical data in different countries on the loss of a huge number of man-hours as a result of nervous breakdown due to psychological incompatibility in the work environment.

Individual style of activity

There are two ways of ensuring the effectiveness of human performance. One is by professional selection, the so-called 'screening out' of individuals with specific attributes. The other is through training methods directed towards the formation of individual strategies of activity that are based on features of the individual's personality. The concept of individual style of activity was first introduced by Soviet psychologists Merlin (1986) and Klimov (1969). They were able to establish that different individuals can perform the same work with equal efficiency by using their own individual style of performance which is more suited to their personalities. The individual style of activity is considered to be a strategy of performance which occurs at the conscious and unconscious levels, deriving from the mechanism of self-regulation (Bedny and Voskoboynikov, 1975; Voskoboynikov, 2014).

Any kind of human activity requires a number of qualities from a person in order to perform. Some personality features relate better to the requirements of the activity, others not so much. People attempt to compensate for their individual weaknesses with their personal strength in a given task situation. Through the individual style of activity people adapt to situations more easily and perform in a more efficient way. This suggests that managers should rely on people's strengths rather than insisting on fixing their weaknesses. As a result, managers will benefit from people's capabilities and will experience satisfaction from their performance.

Communication

The communication process takes place when each party makes an effort to understand what the other party is trying to communicate. In some activities the value of clear communication cannot be overestimated; for example, in communication between pilots and air-traffic controllers. If a command or the confirmation of a command is not understood correctly by either of them, this may lead to serious and sometimes even tragic consequences (Makarov & Voskoboynikov, 2011). In the ordinary, everyday business affairs, clear and proper communication is equally important. The following is an example. In 2009, after the financial crisis of 2005–2007 in the United States, the government launched a programme to help homeowners with their mortgages. Under the programme, banks reduced the interest rate to qualified borrowers, thereby reducing their monthly mortgage payments. The homeowners sighed with relief. But unfortunately that was not the end of the story. In some banks, the department which was offering mortgage relief to homeowners failed to communicate with the department in charge of implementing foreclosure. As a result, there were cases where the foreclosure departments, observing that homeowners were now making lower monthly mortgage payments, assumed that they had defaulted . . . and seized their properties.

Understanding is subjective; it occurs in the receiver's mind. The fact that the communicator transmitted the message and the receiver heard it does not mean that communication has taken place. Even when the receiver has understood the instruction or information the way it is intended to be understood by the communicator, this does not yet constitute a completed communication process. Communication is not only the receipt and understanding of information, it is also an acceptance and action that result from it. This can be illustrated, in a humorous manner, by an episode from the popular US sitcom *Seinfeld*. Jerry Seinfeld and his friend Elaine call a car rental company to reserve a car. When they arrive to pick up the car, they are told that no car is available for them. Jerry begins complaining about the service, to which the receptionist replies with irritation, 'We know how to take a reservation'. Jerry immediately retorts, 'The main thing about reservations is not how to take the reservation, the main thing about reservation is how to ho-o-o-ld the reservation'.

One of the most common blunders of communication in management is when the manager assumes that everything is going well because he did not hear anything to the contrary. Such an assumption is clear evidence of the manager's rare and inefficient communication with subordinates. If subordinates are not getting regular check-ins of their work, they won't know if everything is going in the right direction. If the manager, on the other hand, is not getting regular feedback from subordinates, it will be difficult for him or her to track the progress of the work. Maintaining regular and accurate communication with all the people involved in on-going projects is essential for ensuring the smooth flow of work. That in turn allows anticipating possible missteps and making the necessary corrections in advance. In order to maintain such a business environment managers must provide appropriate and timely information to subordinates, so that they will know what they should do, when they should do it and what is expected from them in general in the framework of the work requirements. In other words, making sure that what is known as 'getting through to people' must take place.

Make them feel important

The late American philosopher John Dewey wrote, 'The deepest urge of human nature is the desire to be important' (as sited in Schul, 1975). It seems that these words were written for managers. When someone makes a person feel important and special, most likely the person experienced the warmest of feelings towards that someone. After that, it is natural to try your very best. To take time outside the office to greet people and make 'small talk' in a friendly and genuine manner will let them know that they are important and valued. People thrive in an atmosphere of acceptance and recognition, and sometimes open up gifts and talents in themselves that were not even suspected.

Two things motivate people more strongly than anything else – achievements, and acknowledgment of achievements by their superiors. People desire recognition, they want to experience their own importance. They want to have their ideas considered and to feel a real sense of accomplishment. The important factor in delivering recognition is to deliver it in a timely fashion, not to wait for some official event to mark the employee's contribution to team success. To make all possible efforts to note people's merits when they expect it is called positive reinforcement, which tends to increase the probability that the act will occur again. Announcing at a meeting that the employee has done something special, or present-ing a handwritten note from a superior, or any other manner of acknowledgment, plays an important role in encouraging employees to continue to perform at their best. Even if the success was achieved mainly because of the manager's own actions, to congratulate people on that achievement plays an important role as well. After all, it is they who have carried out the instructions they received from the manager.

Conclusion

In everyday life each and every one of us uses psychology in dealing with people, even though we are not always consciously aware of that application. We respond to the behaviour of others, we try to predict their reactions and build our relationships on that basis. We are guided by our experience, intuition, conventional wisdom etc. Some do it successfully, others suffer from their blunders. But if a person in a position to manage other people's activity makes blunders, they suffer from it too. The more people that are under his or her command, the higher the cost of that person's psychological illiteracy to the organisation or business and to society as a whole.

References

Bedny, G. Z. & Voskoboynikov, F. A. (1975). Problems of how a person adapts to the objective requirements of activity. In V. G. Aseev (Ed.), *Psychological problems of personality* (Vol. 2) (pp. 18–30). Irkutsk: Irkutsk University Press.

Klimov, E. (1969). *Individual style of activity.* Kazan: Kazan University Press.

Makarov, R. & Voskoboynikov, F. (2011) Methodology for teaching flight-specific English to nonnative English-speaking air-traffic controllers. In G. Z. Bedny and W. Karwowski (Eds), *Human–computer interaction and operator' performance* (pp. 277–304). Boca Raton, FL: Taylor & Francis Group.

Merlin, W. (1986). *Outlines of integral study of individuality.* Moscow: Pedagogy.

Schul, B. D. (1975). *How to be an effective group leader.* Chicago: Nelson-Hall.

Voskoboynikov, F. (2014). The influence of personality features on performance in work, study and athletic activity. In T. Marek, W. Karwowski, M. Frankewicz, J. Kantola and P. Zgaga (Eds), *Human factor of a global society: A system of systems perspective* (pp. 187–192). Boca Raton, FL: Taylor & Francis Group.

Voskoboynikov, F. (2017). *The psychology of effective management: Strategy of relationship building.* New York: Routledge.

Wallace, A. (1960, 11 December). Morris Viteles, industrial psychologist. *Philadelphia Enquirer*, p. 29.

3

Requirements

A PRIMER ON PROJECT REQUIREMENTS MANAGEMENT

Darren Dalcher

Projects typically arise in response to the needs, wants or wishes of an individual, group, organisation or community. Project management endeavours to capture, analyse, prioritise, justify and transform these needs and wants into desired outputs and outcomes that deliver and deploy the required functionality, or performance, to the target community.

The conceptual steps that lead to the transformation from a concept or need into a more formal form of a systems requirements document are addressed through the processes of requirements management. Fittingly, the sixth edition of the *APM Body of Knowledge,* published by the UK's Association for Project Management (APM), defines requirements management as 'the process of capturing, assessing and justifying stakeholders' wants and needs' (APM, 2012, p. 140). This chapter looks at the activities and processes that underpin requirements management, and the issues and challenges that emerge from its use.

Requirements management is concerned with understanding, formulating and documenting the perceived needs of stakeholders. Before focusing on requirements management, it is essential to gain an appreciation of the role of needs in forming and informing requirements and of the role of needs analysis as the essential precursor to requirements management.

Needs analysis

Most endeavours begin with a need which is then elaborated and actualised. At a fundamental level, projects are devised to satisfy needs. The APM definition of requirements management talks about capturing stakeholder needs as well as assessing and justifying them; however, very little is normally said about needs and their identification and management.

Determining needs is never simple: it involves analysts intimately collaborating with users, clients and stakeholders. One of the crucial skills for analysts involved in needs analysis is the ability to distinguish between needs and wants.

A need is said to emerge from an unfulfilled desire, or an idea for improvement for some part of a system. Needs imply a desire to solve a problem, improve the status quo, meet a business objective, satisfy a legal stipulation or correct a deficiency in current arrangements. This can be done through the provision of new functionality, delivery of new assets or acquisition of new performance capabilities. At its most basic level, a need can be viewed as a gap between current results, and desired results and consequences. A key point is to express it as a gap that may pertain to a problem (and hence a noun), and not in terms of a potential solution.

Wants typically relate to the wishes of an individual or a stakeholder group and their expectations related to a system or project. While needs relate to the absolute essentials that one has to have, wants are not absolutely necessary, as they represent the things that one would like to have. Wants extend beyond needs to reveal the additional wishes and expectations of users and stakeholders. It is worth pointing out that wants can be unlimited; when one want is satisfied, another often arises as expectations are raised. Wants are also context dependent and may vary in time, depending on situational contingencies.

Given that there will inevitably be multiple needs and wants, and that the resources and projects available to implement these are limited, it is important to determine the essential nature of what is required and why it is required, as well as who requires it. The main purpose is to establish beyond doubt that there is a recognised need that will require supporting and addressing. The discussion of solutions is deferred to later stages, so needs analysis is always done independently from preconceived resolution options, as by definition it relates to the actual needs.

Understanding the needs of users and stakeholders is an essential precursor to determining their requirements. Before requirements can be elicited and developed, it is essential to have a well-defined problem where the needs or gaps are clearly understood. Stating problems in a clear and unambiguous manner is a crucial art that enables the right problem to be solved. Focusing on problems rather than solutions allows the measurement of the utility of a given solution against the original needs to determine the degree of satisfaction achieved.

Stakeholders may be stimulated by shortcomings in current capability or systems, or be inspired by the performance of new technology in other areas, which can make new systems and projects possible. It is crucial to understand each need, its origin and its implications before proceeding with a project. Indeed, Frame (2003) asserts that the emergence of needs sets off the whole project process.

New capabilities must first be recognised by stakeholders so that they can be evaluated in context. The essential context is defined by the scope of the project; however, needs analysis may point to areas and facets not included in the scope and may help to form a better picture of the essential issues that need to be considered, occasionally forcing a reconsideration of the scope or real dimensions of change. Indeed, many change projects would benefit from extending their scope to consider external business events that relate to the core function of proposed projects. In other words, the boundary drawn around an environment or context can be crucial to how change is viewed and what is deemed possible.

Needs evolve from a vague idea or concept to something tangible that ultimately underpins and directs entire endeavours and projects, yet they also lead to the emergence of constraints and limitations. They are assessed prior to the consideration of any solution so as to allow the exploration to lead to real requirements and avoid premature selection of or influence by a predetermined solution.

Frame (2003) identifies three main stages related to the development of needs: emergence, recognition and articulation. This is shown pictorially in Figure 3.1.

- *Needs emergence*: Needs are dynamic, altering with time. They arise and materialise out of change. The availability of technology, the growth in social participation, global markets and the accelerating rate of change incite new needs, whilst altering existing ones. New needs and expectations can appear inside the organisation or be stimulated by external changes introduced by competitors, or be induced by changes in the external environments.
- *Needs recognition*: Systematic identification of needs requires regular return visits to the needs and expectations of an organisation, its stakeholders and its customers to assess their current needs against the previously recognised set. Attention to anticipated needs in the marketplace can help in planning future initiatives and projects.
- *Needs articulation*: The meaning and implications of needs are important. Articulation implies an in-depth study of a need. The attempt to describe the essence of a need requires a deeper understanding of the roots of a need, its fine details and true meaning and the implications that it may have. Developing and recording that understanding paves the way to developing the requirements. Once a need is truly understood and carefully articulated, it forms the basis for requirements elicitation, as stipulating what needs to be done to meet it becomes significantly simpler.

Needs analysis is focused on stakeholders and their goals, aspirations and needs with regard to any improvements. Needs analysis requires the identification of users and stakeholders, the articulation of their goals, and the identification, recognition and articulation of needs and gaps.

The techniques applied draw upon stakeholder engagement and management, emphasising stakeholder identification and stakeholder mapping, whilst particularly focusing on identifying interests and charting influences that play a key part in determining the expectations of different stakeholder groups. As was proposed

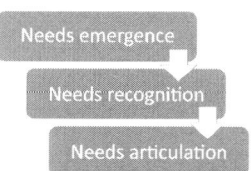

FIGURE 3.1 Project needs life cycle

above, systems methods that explore the boundaries of systems and the relevant context are also essential in identifying and exploring issues and positioning projects to address the key aspects required to deliver the change pointed to through the articulated needs. Enterprise modelling methods and business analysis techniques can also play a part in analysing the as-is enterprise and in determining limitations and identifying deficiencies with respect to the recorded needs. The work completed during needs analysis serves as the preparation for determining, developing and specifying the requirements.

Defining requirements

Articulated needs serve as the basis for formulating the plans for the project in terms of the agreed aspects that need to be represented in the proposed system. This calls for transforming the defined needs into a set of requirements that will underpin the project.

A requirement is a statement that identifies a condition, function or capability needed by a stakeholder in order to solve a problem or achieve an objective. It is alternatively defined as a condition or capability that MUST be met in order to satisfy a contract, standard, specification or some formally imposed document. In some contexts, a requirement may refer to a documented representation of such a condition or capability. While there are many alternative definitions, it is clear that requirements can represent the current or future state of any aspect of an enterprise, particularly in the context of an articulated and clearly specified need.

It is important to distinguish between user requirements and system require-ments. Initially analysts will work with different stakeholders to refine the needs statements into what is known as *user requirements*. User requirements are captured in a random order, and are clearly focused on the needs of different stakeholders. An increasing trend is to develop the requirements collaboratively with the relevant stakeholders. Sharing and collaboration activities serve to provide greater insight and understanding of what is truly needed. Analysts are thus concerned with turning noisy, unstructured information from users into measurable, testable user requirements that will form the foundation for all subsequent system work. The format of user requirements is simple, so that they are understandable and clear to the users and can thus be used as the basis for agreement and negotiation.

However, the statements made by users and stakeholders are often not sufficiently useful for other developers and professionals. User requirements are short and non-technical, yet are often stated in terms of a solution. The purpose of user requirements is to derive a deeper understanding of the needs, and therefore analysts will endeavour to refine them by focusing on needs rather than solutions. Analysts act as the interface between the different communities engaged in project work. *Systems requirements* evolve from user requirements to define what the system must do to meet the needs. Their role is to assist other professionals further downstream (who will likely not have the benefit of interrogating the different stakeholder groups) by providing a definitive statement of what is needed. System requirements explore the solution in terms of 'what' is needed (not 'how' it might be delivered).

User requirements are akin to expanding the needs assessment described above, while systems requirements are primarily concerned with the development of a working specification that captures the essence of what is needed (and why), and how achievement can be measured. The processes and activities required to deliver this working document are described below.

Types of requirements

We often hear about functional requirements, but in practice there are a number of different types of requirements that will need to be collected and stated. The following classification scheme shows the many different general types of requirements and the diverse concerns they embody.

Classification scheme for requirements

Business requirements: Higher-level statements of the goals, objectives, conditions or needs of the enterprise. They may, for example, describe the reasons why a specific project has been initiated, the objectives that it will achieve and the proposed measurements to determine its success. Business requirements emerge from *enterprise analysis* and relate to the entire organisation, rather than to specific business units or stakeholder groups, and may therefore apply across multiple projects. (Note: some organisations will use the term 'enterprise requirements' to capture wider organisational issues, reserving the term 'business requirements' to the specific requirements raised by business users. An alternative approach is to split business requirements into the subcategories of strategic, tactical and operational requirements).

Stakeholder requirements: Statement of needs of a particular stakeholder or class of stakeholders. They will typically specify how that stakeholder will interact with a solution and specify their performance needs and expectations. Stakeholder requirements are elicited and formalised through requirements analysis.

Solution requirements: The technical characteristics of the solution that meets the business requirements and stakeholder requirements. They are identified and refined through requirements analysis and include:

- **Functional requirements**, describing the essential behaviour and capabilities of the system in terms of operation or responses. These are derived from the fundamental purpose of the product (i.e. the needs it satisfies).
- **Non-functional requirements**, describing environmental conditions under which the solution must remain effective. These may relate to quality capabilities, such as availability, capacity and speed. Non-functional

requirements, also known as quality-of-service requirements, may also refer to design and management constraints, which are likely to emerge at each phase of the life cycle where additional detail is obtained. Non-functional requirements may also encompass:

- o   Look and feel requirements, describing the appearance
- o   Environmental requirements, describing the location and conditions
- o   Usability requirements, identifying ease of use
- o   Performance requirements
- o   Operational requirements
- o   Product requirements, identifying key attributes in the product
- o   Maintainability requirements
- o   Security requirements
- o   Political requirements, encompassing culture and politics
- o   Legal requirements
- o   Information requirements, including privacy
- o   Interface requirements, detailing attributes related to interacting or communication
- o   Regulatory requirements imposed by relevant regulators
- o   Organisational requirements, including applicable broad policies and procedures that apply to the contracting or contractor organisations
- o   Ethical requirements
- o   Future-proofing requirements that enable growth in capacity and potential in response to anticipated trends and emerging technologies
- o   Training requirements.

Transition requirements: The specific capabilities required to facilitate transition from the current state to a desired future state. These are temporary requirements that may relate to skill gaps to be addressed or to specific migration and conversion of data and will emerge from the solution assessment and validation activities.

Functional requirements would thus represent the characteristics of the outputs of a project which delivers the solution. These will hopefully address the stakeholder requirements and needs, while respecting and supporting the business requirements. Transition requirements would enable the delivery and implementation of the solution.

In reality, the distinction between the different types is some times blurred; none the less, the classification is useful in identifying the different types of requirements whilst providing a useful tool for highlighting the different perspectives that may be usefully considered.

Tip: Requirements that do not appear to be independent and that may seem to relate to more than one of the classes, may merit further investigation to determine and untangle the relationships and dependencies. It is often the case that such requirements harbour assumptions and unidentified concerns that can be unpacked into individual and independent statements.

Requirements acquisition activities

Requirements serve as the foundation for developing solutions and delivering projects. Requirements statements therefore need to be complete, concise, clear, correct and consistent. However, requirements cannot simply be collected, as they very often appear to be poorly stated, inconsistent, incomplete and ambiguous; instead, a number of interconnected activities begin with more systematic elicitation of requirements from relevant stakeholders, clients and users. A combination of techniques is normally used to develop the richness and multiplicity of perspectives and viewpoints.

The activities often require cycles of interaction between the analysts and the stakeholders attempting to describe their needs and the proposed external behaviour of the system by focusing on what needs to be done and formulating the evaluation criteria. In this way the need is elaborated through a process of questioning the stakeholder and formulating the problem gap into a clearly understood area of agreement. The full set of activities is discussed below.

Elicitation

Requirements elicitation is concerned with obtaining further information related to the diverse needs, perspectives and expectations of different stakeholder groups. Elicitation relies on a variety of techniques, including: brainstorming, interviews, focus groups, Delphi technique, requirements workshops, observation, document analysis, surveys/questionnaires, market research, interface analysis, form analysis, task analysis, scenario analysis, domain analysis, business process redesign, prototyping, story-boarding, ethnography, role playing, analysis of natural language, stories and narrative methods. How much of the requirements are known is critical to selecting the most suitable approach: the real art of elicitation is in selecting the methods that will work with a particular group and identifying their needs. Elicitation and continuing engagement with stakeholder groups is likely to lead to further requirements and refinements. Once sufficient detail has been recorded, it is expected that the requirements analysis phase will begin, possibly in parallel with elicitation.

Analysis

Requirements analysis is concerned with assessment and classification of the elicited requirements to define the required capabilities that will fulfil the identified stakeholder needs. It is concerned with the interrelationships between requirements and the relative importance of each. The analysis will therefore encompass the stakeholder' needs to determine if these are represented, as well as the solution requirements, which identify the essential characteristics and behaviours required to describe a solution in sufficient detail to allow it to be designed, implemented and reviewed for achievement following release.

Organisation

Requirements organisation classifies requirements into a set of views, perspectives, profiles or roles. Each organised grouping will be comprehensive, complete and consistent from all stakeholder perspectives and enable the identification of inter-elationships and dependencies. Structuring and organising is often useful in questioning the basis and links between requirements, and can often uncover hierarchical or related considerations that will result in uncovering further requirements.

Allocation

Requirements allocation is an iterative process that includes allocation and apportionment of requirements to functional elements. This is often done through systematic decomposition of systems requirements, generating a lower-level requirements structure. Whilst it is a requirements activity it is closely linked to traceability.

Prioritisation (and negotiation)

Requirements prioritisation is concerned with creating new ways of working in response to the needs. Most requirements are negotiable and need to be considered in light of other requirements. Prioritisation ensures that both analysis and project implementation are focused on the most important or most relevant requirements. This is often done through prioritisation indices, decision-making models, utility allocations or very simple prioritisation tools that identify the must haves, should haves, could haves and won't haves, or look to designate labels such as: essential, desirable or optional.

The requirements prioritisation process is used to decide which requirements need to be addressed. The prioritisation process depends on negotiation, decision making and trade-offs between priorities, values, viewpoints, expectations, risks and urgency, or some other agreed criteria. By the end of the activity each requirement should have an assigned priority. It is worth noting that some requirements may not merit a high ranking for their own value but may be needed to support other requirements or to implement regulatory or governance aspects, which may take precedence over the concern of other stakeholder groups.

Project negotiation is also likely to be included, where conflicting priorities and requirements are untangled in order to resolve identified conflicts. Prioritisation will determine which subset of the requirements can be allocated to a specific project whilst considering the specific characteristics, constraints and stakeholder viewpoints that need addressing. Conversely, the process can also be used to allocate different priorities to the entire collection of requirements, which will enable agile method to develop a portfolio of requirements suited to each timebox.

Specification

The ultimate result of the requirements activities is the creation of an explicit refined specification or model of the system's requirements in a technical language. This document describes the external characteristics required in any proposed solution that is likely to address the identified needs. The requirements specification reflects the agreed understanding of the steps to be taken (or the problem requiring resolution) and often adds technical details required by designers and engineers further downstream. In other words, it provides a technical specification or a blue-print of what is to be found in the solution (but not of how it will be designed). It is likely to be used as the basis for a contract, as a means of communicating the agreement and sharing it with other professionals (such as designers, architects and project managers) and as a way of measuring compliance with the contract.

Following completion, the delivered system or project is likely to be tested against this definition to ensure compliance with the specification. Ultimately the requirements specification will serve as the gateway to the rest of the project, or life cycle. Note that the statement specifies the characteristics required but avoids making any reference to a particular solution. The adoption of the requirements specification often marks the beginning of the detailed search for an adequate solution. A good requirements specification would contain sufficient information in order to satisfy stakeholders' needs, and nothing more.

Verification

Requirements verification ensures that requirements are stated correctly, completely and consistently. The activity also confirms that the model meets the necessary standards of quality and warrants that the requirements have been defined correctly. Verification is done by utilising rules to establish, check and confirm each model and statement.

Validation

Requirements validation ensures that the correct requirements are stated. The intention is to prove that all requirements meet a stakeholder value, satisfy a need and/or deliver value to the business, and also to confirm that stakeholder, project solution and execution are aligned. According to Davis (2005), a valid requirement must pass two tests; namely, the satisfaction of the requirement must be externally observable, and it must help to fulfil a recognised stakeholder need.

Formal acceptance

Requirements acceptance marks the commitment of a requirement to a requirements baseline with a formal signoff to ensure that only controlled changes will be allowed from this point onwards. Requirements management activities will be concerned with maintaining and evolving the baseline during development.

The requirements management process

Not all requirements activities are done early on during the development process: requirements tasks typically span the entire project life cycle. Indeed requirements are assumed to be always active and would benefit from progressive elaboration. Moreover, they need to be kept up to date throughout development. A useful way of thinking about the process is to view requirements as a form of retained knowledge. This perspective encourages requirements to be considered as a project, and even an organisational resource, thereby justifying investment and attention.

Some projects dedicate 5 per cent of the development resources to requirements-related activities. As a rule of thumb it is recognised that 10 per cent is a more reasonable figure, given the range of activities called upon. Empirical research suggests that projects dedicating less than 8 per cent to requirements have a significantly higher likelihood of failing than those in the range of 10–15 per cent. Hood et al. (2008) suggest that on the basis of 'best practice', 40 per cent of development time should be allocated to requirements and specification activities, but the range of 10–12 per cent is more typical in many sectors and industries.

While some people talk about using a requirements management process, the fact is that in reality the steps alternate and change between the different activities, with some progressing in parallel. Many books describe them as a cycle, a wheel or simply a set of connected activities progressing in parallel. The key certainties are that, following identification of the needs, the initial step is requirements elicitation. Indeed, the process related to the development of a requirements specification is iterative by nature and feedback-driven. The pace is uneven, as some activities generate further requirements, with activities revisited several times. In traditional projects, these iterations will mostly precede the design activities. In agile processes and projects, iteration and feedback will be accommodated as part of the development cycles and fit within designated timeboxes.

Gaps and contradictions may be identified later in the process, and these can be explored using the same methods and key activities. For example, missing, incorrect and incomplete requirements will be identified during the analysis phase which may necessitate additional elicitation. Other iterations and cycling-through activities are also possible until the requirements are deemed to be complete.

Davis (2005) points out that requirements are transformed from the beginning of elicitation to the end of the requirements specification in a wide variety of ways, including:

- agreement: change from suggestions to a fully agreed consensus by all parties;
- completeness: more and more requirements are added as we think about the process;

- detail: change from relatively abstract statements to detailed and considered statements;
- precision: the initial stages tolerate ambiguity, which is reduced as the process progresses;
- augmentation: the initial sentences are augmented with models, pictures, annotations, explanations, supporting evidence and cross-references.

The gap between the starting point of the process, and the end result has also been described as the difference between 'stated requirements' uttered at the beginning of the process and the 'real requirements' that evolve from the stated requirements during the requirements acquisition activities (Young, 2006).

The next section looks at the activities and infrastructure required to support the management of requirements during the requirements phases and beyond into the rest of the project.

Managing requirements

This section is concerned with the supporting activities underpinning the management of requirements throughout development and management. Many quality procedures and supporting mechanisms are employed to enable and maintain the requirements.

Requirements repository

Changes to requirements have to be recorded and managed. Failure to document or track proposed requirements means they might not be utilised. A requirements repository is often used to store requirements, including: approved requirements, requirements under development and requirements under review. A system for adding, changing and deleting requirements is normally established. Each individual requirement is likely to have a unique means of identification, which will also be utilised in showing conflicts and demonstrating traceability and linkages. Good requirements will include the following attributes: date, source (or origin of the requirement), its rationale, priority, status and version.

Assumptions

It is also extremely useful to record assumptions. Different people make different assumptions, and where assumptions surface during the elicitation or elaboration process, it is important to identify them. Assumptions can be used during risk assessment. They can be investigated during the prioritisation and their impact can be decoupled from the relevant requirement during the requirement specification phase.

Baselines and signoff

Agreed and approved requirements will be baselined following a formal signoff as described above. However, it is naïve to assume that changes will stop following signoff: requirements will change and new knowledge regarding them will emerge. Failure to respond to required changes is likely to lead to obsolete products or project failure. Instead there is a need to develop systems so that all proposed changes can be considered and authorised by the change control board and recorded by the configuration management system.

In many projects requirements are in a constant state of flux, requiring changes and updates. In some projects it is not recommended to attempt to freeze the requirements too early in the life cycle as there is a need to allow for conflict resolution and omissions. Similarly, it is not possible to keep changing forever, as this is likely to lead to requirements creep. The ideal position is somewhere between the two states as reflected in Figure 3.2. To the left of the line (as we move towards the y-axis) it is too easy to freeze the requirements, while movement to the right, towards the x-axis, would represent requirements creep.

Configuration control

All requirements are placed under formal change control. Change management processes are used to authorise changes to requirements and will take into account cost and effort estimates and indication of the expected impact of each change, as well as the relevant benefits and risk. Refinement, corrections and filling in of detail that is uncovered during the process will thus be informed by calculations of impact, risk and importance, which can be fed back to the relevant stakeholder groups and used to manage expectations.

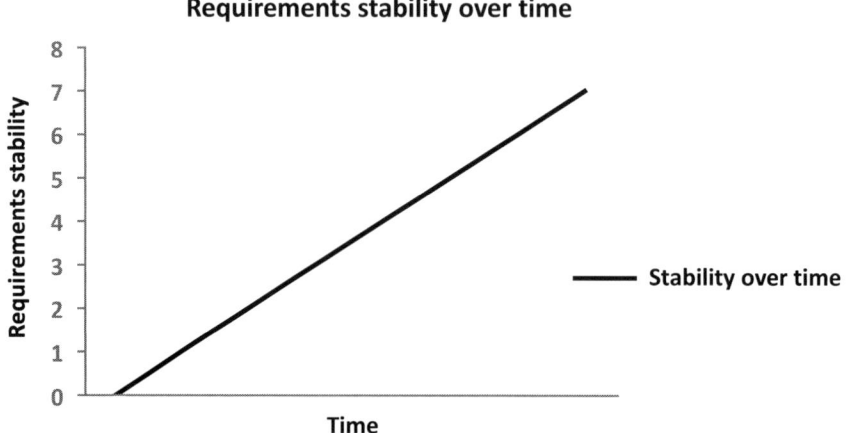

FIGURE 3.2 Requirements stability over time

Traceability

Tracing requirements back to the business goals and objectives helps in validating whether a requirement should be included. Traceability is also used in requirements breakdown structures to keep track of essential requirements and ensure that they are properly broken down into sub-requirements that are addressed at lower levels. It also aids in limiting scope creep and agreeing on the essential activities required to successfully deliver the project, whilst ensuring that all aspects are covered and no new ones appear without notice. In that sense traceability provides a book-keeping system for essential requirements. Moreover, traceability provides a way of linking those requirements to stakeholders and their recorded needs, and to other artefacts and requirements.

Traceability also plays a key part in ensuring conformance to requirements, a recognised quality measure, whilst underpinning scope, risk, cost and change management activities. Traceability is closely linked to requirements allocation and flow-down through functional decomposition, and flow-up to validation of needs. Tools that support these aspects include traceability lists, the requirements traceability matrix, traceability manuals and the mapping of requirements to project scope and to work breakdown structure deliverables, as well as mapping requirements to test cases.

Testing

It is important to define the evaluation criteria early on. Testability can be established during requirements elicitation by focusing on the fit criterion. The fit criterion is a measurement of the requirements that enables testers to precisely determine whether the system meets (or fits) the requirement. So, a requirement for confirming the identity of each customer immediately may be rewritten as: 'Client identity records must be displayed within 10 seconds of an identity request being logged.' Fit criteria provide a way of establishing clear-cut acceptance tests for each requirement (Robertson and Robertson, 2012).

Accountability

Requirements accountability is concerned with ensuring that all requirements have been allocated and addressed.

Future-proofing

Needs analysis and requirements assessment activities are likely to uncover future needs, and requirements that are unlikely to be of use beyond the current project. These can be recorded, tracked and allocated to future projects. It is a useful exercise from an organisational perspective.

Key success factors for project requirements

The ten key success factors for delivering good requirements are the following.

- Initiate your requirements management effort by focusing on needs.
- Identify all relevant stakeholders to determine the needs to be fulfilled.
- Select experienced requirements analysts and experts (and develop them).
- Foster the development of a collaborative environment for cooperation.
- Map requirements against the needs they fulfil.
- Establish objective testing criteria to prove the achievement of needs.
- Allow requirements to evolve, where needed.
- Use the requirements as a way of communicating with the stakeholder groups.
- Allow time and resources for the requirements activities.
- Establish clear support from the project manager for the requirements effort.

Communicating requirements

Requirements communication is increasingly used to ensure that all stakeholders have a shared understanding of the proposed project. It is useful in setting and managing the expectations of stakeholders and in maintaining their involvement. It is also a useful tool in reaching agreement about the approach and the key requirements that will be used as a test to determine if the delivered project meets the intended requirements.

If there are multiple stakeholder groups, the communication process will involve identifying their specific interests and developing appropriate formats for presenting the requirements that suit each group and enable it to engage with the project. This is made easier through working it back to the needs statement developed for the different groups.

Business analysis increasingly relies on securing the approval of key stakeholder groups as a tool for managing the scope of the project and the solution concept that will implement the agreed requirements.

The following section focuses on writing good requirements.

Writing effective requirements

Requirements are not written by project management experts; instead, they are researched and compiled by analysts engaged in an intensive, highly interactive and collaborative process. Poor handling of requirements results in problems further down the line. The key skills associated with the role include excellent communication skills, strong stakeholder focus, knowledge of business analysis or a similar domain, organisational research skills and a variety of soft and interpersonal skills. Additional expertise normally includes facilitation and conflict resolution.

Some guidelines on how to write effective requirements are offered below.

Requirements should not identify or focus on a potential solution; they should instead refer to the need and what it means. In order to try to avoid the temptation of thinking about the implementation or a particular solution, the writing is normally focused on what is needed, rather than how it might be delivered.

The writing style is factual. Good requirements tend to use 'shall', while statements of fact will make use of 'will' and goals are described in terms of 'should'.

Additional guidelines used in requirements specification include the following.

- Use a unique identifier for each new requirement.
- Avoid undefined words such as best, ideal, optimal, easy, sufficient, adequate, quick, rapid, inexpensive, informed, improved, enhanced, supportive, user-friendly.
- Avoid ambiguous measures such as some, several, many, few.
- Clearly identify units of measure next to numbers (i.e. make it clear if it is four seconds, minutes, hours or days).
- Avoid absolute terms such as: always, never, all.
- Do not use complicated conjunctions such as: if, when, but, except, unless and although.
- Avoid using terms such as usually, normally, typically, frequently, occasionally, generally, scarcely, hardly and often.
- Avoid using terms such as obviously, clearly, certainly.
- Consider carefully whether words such as downloaded, processed and accessed are specific enough.
- Resist the temptation to use etc. and so on . . .
- Some common terms such as efficient, effective, minimise and maximise are difficult to use in requirements specifications.

Finally, it is worth ensuring that all TBD or TBC entries (to be determined/to be confirmed) have been cleared and the real aspects are included in the requirement as soon as possible. A final check prior to signoff is strongly advised.

SMART requirements

In order to write effective requirements, it is often suggested that a revised version of SMART is used to challenge and fine-tune each requirement in turn. SMART, initially introduced by Doran (1981), is an acronym where each letter refers to a task in the process of elaborating a clearer definition. By working through the statement using one line of SMART at a time, it becomes possible to elaborate a quality requirement.

The following is a slightly revised, and somewhat longer, version of SMARTTT for requirements.

Specific	Be specific and precise.
Measurable	Establish a measurable indicator of progress.
Assignable	Is agreed by and can be associated with a stakeholder.
Realistic	Can be realistically achieved within constraints.

Time related	Using a specific timeframe.
Traceable	Full traceability to needs, stakeholder and test.
Testable	Define test criteria to confirm achievement.

Criteria for a good requirement

The quality attributes or criteria for determining the qualities of a good requirement normally include the following.

Complete: self-contained, without omissions, covering all significant aspects.
Cohesive: supports purpose and scope.
Concise: brief and to the point.
Consistent: same content regardless of format; different parts do not conflict.
Correct: free of errors and satisfying a need.
Feasible: technically, as well as within time, cost and resource constraints.
Modifiable: necessary changes can be accommodated.
Necessary: needed.
Ranked: ordered and prioritised.
Readable: by the right community.
Testable: verifiable; fulfilment can be proven.
Traceable: origin and rationale are visible.
Unambiguous: only one interpretation is possible.
Understandable: by the right communities.

The criteria can be used as a checklist against individual requirements. It is worth noting that some of the attributes are difficult to measure. The value of the list therefore is in forming a view of what would make a good requirement and using it as a quality test, where possible.

Why requirements management is needed

There are many reasons why requirements are crucial to the success of projects. Information captured during requirements acquisition feeds directly into the activities of bid writing, contracting, project planning and scheduling, risk management, trade-offs, decision making, project monitoring, acceptance testing, performance management, quality management, change control and reporting. They also feed into the contract and procurement cycles and can be useful in expectation management, relationship management, managing partnerships and, most fundamentally, can underpin communication.

Undoubtedly, requirements should underpin many management activities and concerns, whilst providing a sound basis for subsequent activities. The rest of this section will view requirements through a variety of perspectives, and roles that they enable.

Requirements as a map: A key purpose of the requirements is to provide a blueprint for the development of the project and the required artefacts. The process and resulting documentation are designed to give a better idea about what needs to be done, and how to get there, whilst providing detailed information about the technical aspects. The remainder of the process can be informed and guided by the documented requirements.

Requirements as a test: Continuing with the journey analogy, it also provides a means of determining whether the journey has been completed successfully by establishing the specific criteria, or the yardstick, required to test the satisfaction of the stated needs and the achievement of the required functionalities and capabilities.

Requirements as a decision point: The requirements provide managers with a natural go/no-go gateway at the beginning of the development and delivery process.

Requirements as insight: The processes of needs assessment and requirement management provide analysts, developers and managers with insights into the issues and concerns of various stakeholder communities. They also enable stakeholders working together with analysts to make better sense of their context and real requirements.

Requirements as communication: The process of identifying needs and eliciting requirements provides a mechanism for engaging with the various stakeholder communities. Intermediate products and statements offer a means and mechanism for facilitating discussion and fostering agreement.

Requirements as a contract: Requirements can be used as the contract that underpins further development. They are often used as a proof of concept and as evidence that developers understand what needs to be done.

Requirements as agreement: Requirements involve negotiation and trade-off between multiple communities, stakeholders, preferences, viewpoints and perspectives. The artefacts employed during the process provide the interface needed to view different positions and reach agreement, documenting the common understanding. The collaborative process of teasing out and ranking the requirements becomes an effective tool for stakeholder engagement and for managing the expectations of the diverse stakeholder communities.

Requirements as management: Managing the set of requirements enables projects to maintain focus on the key needs and agreed requirements. Mapping the requirements offers greater visibility into the activities and processes required in managing the project.

Requirements as quality: Requirements management ensures that the correct system is being built. One of the definitions of quality relates to conformance to requirements. Specifying requirements with test criteria allows the establishment of measures that can be used in measuring the quality of projects and deliverables.

Requirements as history: Requirements provide a historical record of how an idea or concept came into being.

Requirements as interface: Requirements provide a link between business objectives, stakeholder needs, proposed improvements and specific projects. They provide traceability from specific endeavours to organisational priorities and back to stakeholder concerns, and thus carry, facilitate, record and enable communication and sharing across different levels, communities and concerns.

And the counter-case: why we cannot do without it

The consequences of wrong, incomplete or messy requirements are rejection of the system by stakeholders whose needs have not been addressed, the need to retrofit and make corrections to released systems, loss of confidence and reputation, loss of money and the potential for ultimate project failure.

Young (2006) points out that requirements errors account for the largest class of errors typically found in a project, using examples of between 41–56 per cent of errors discovered overall. Other evidence also identifies a range of 40–60 per cent. The figures suggest that the greatest impact can be accomplished by correcting, or not making, errors during the requirements activities. Additional effort invested in improving the requirements process may prove a cost-effective investment.

Requirements determination is a particularly volatile phase, as requirements are unearthed during the initiation phases when the level of uncertainty about the project is at its greatest (Figure 3.3, mouth of the cone showing the greatest degree of variance). Accurate estimates can be made when the requirements are understood and agreed. Offering a greater degree of confidence in what needs to be addressed, and what the financial implications might be. The sooner a mutual understanding of the project is achieved, the greater the likelihood of deriving correct products, reflective plans and accurate estimates.

It is now generally accepted in project management that the cost to effect changes and correct errors increases dramatically as the project progresses (Figure

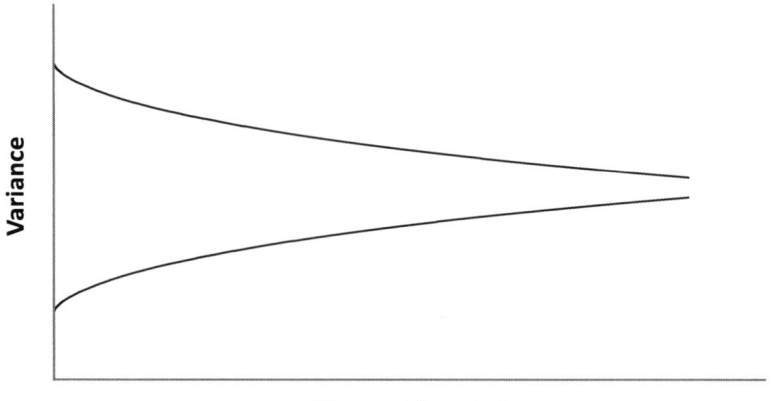

Time or Knowledge

FIGURE 3.3 Cone of uncertainty surrounding a project

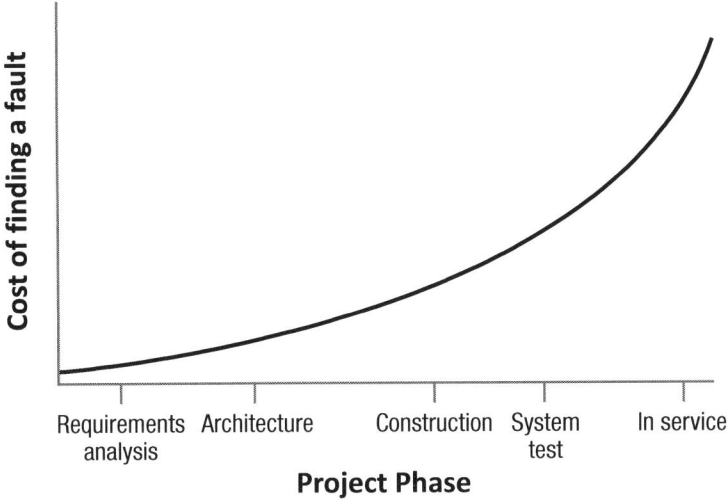

FIGURE 3.4 The relative cost to fix a problem as a function of time

3.4). When errors are found later in the life cycle they cost significantly more to trace, address, re-do and integrate. Discovery during acceptance testing will typically cost between 30 and 70 times the cost of correcting the same error during requirements analysis and specification, while correction when the system is operational would fit in the range of a factor of 40–1000.

The relative cost of correcting errors is a function dependent on the phase during which they are corrected. The cheapest and easiest time to make changes is early in the process, when their effects can still be modelled on paper. From a monetary perspective, the ability to cost-effectively control the outcome of the project decreases rapidly in accordance with the life-cycle phase. Consequently, reducing requirements errors and investing additional time and resources in finding and correcting errors and omissions early on constitute the single most effective course of action that developers and managers can take to mitigate failures and improve project outcomes.

Requirements activities do not fall within the remit of project management. Requirements elicitation, analysis, prioritisation and specification require specialist skills which are normally provided by systems analysts, business analysts, requirements analysts, business process re-engineering specialists, enterprise architects or requirements engineers. However, they clearly impact on project outcomes and therefore should constitute a key concern for project managers.

The Standish Group has been tracking the reason for project failures for almost two decades. It regularly publishes the top ten reasons for project failure. The 2010 Standish Report identifies the top ten factors (Table 3.1). The second column shows which of the factors relate to requirements management, with a double tick representing a direct impact and a single tick an area that might be improved as

TABLE 3.1 Top ten reasons for projects to be challenged

Reasons for project to be challenged	Relation to requirements
Lack of user input	2
Incomplete requirements and specification	2
Changing requirements and specification	2
Lack of executive support	1
Technology incompetence	0
Lack of resources	0
Unrealistic expectations	2
Unclear objectives	1
Unrealistic timeframes	0
New technology	0

a result of greater attention to requirements management. The table indicates that requirements management issues have a clear impact on the outcome and potential failure of projects, as major impacts can be identified across at least four of the ten items, with some impact indicated for at least one additional factor. Hull, Jackson and Dick (2011) show a similar exercise for earlier results of the survey: factors related to failures in requirements management practice account for 51.6 per cent of the reasons for project failure, whilst successful requirements management practices also appear to be associated with 42 per cent of the factors identified as leading to success.

Requirements management clearly plays a key part in the success or failure of projects and therefore merits more attention from the project management community. Young (2006) contends that project managers can provide the focus for requirements activities by:

1   setting a high standard for project requirements, demanding and facilitating good requirements analysis, and not accepting inferior requirements;
2   receiving support from project manager for requirements work, including a greater proportion of project resources;
3   using the requirements, assumptions and risks that emerge from the elicitation and analysis activities to shape and refine project plans;
4   ensuring that the right requirements practices, methods and approaches are deployed according to the type of project;
5   'working behind the scenes' to ensure that all relevant stakeholders are iden- tified and influencing them to support and participate in the requirements activities.

Given the importance of requirements activities, we might add an additional require- ment:

- employing experienced and well-qualified analysts to support and underpin the discovery, communication and management of better requirements that will underpin successful projects.

Identifying excellent analysts with communication and facilitation skills will be a good first step towards improving the track record of dealing with requirements.

Difficulties associated with needs and requirements

It would be useful to identify the key difficulties and hurdles associated with instituting and executing requirements management activities in the context of projects. The difficulties are classified into stakeholder issues; environmental issues; requirements process issues; requirements issues (focused on the product); human concerns; and analyst issues.

Stakeholder issues

- Need for stakeholder involvement (and their time availability)
- Ability to articulate needs
- Multiplicity of viewpoints and perspectives
- Conflicting needs
- Need to reconcile needs of different stakeholder groups
- Non-negotiable demands
- Ranking all needs as high priority
- Changing needs
- Changing stakeholders

Environmental issues

- Ill-defined system boundaries
- Poor understanding of the problem domain
- Conflicting priorities
- Changing needs
- Rapidly changing requirements (aka requirements volatility)
- Fragmented information
- Power and politics

Requirements process issues

- Identifying and involving all stakeholder groups
- Confusing wants and needs
- Addressing the needs of the wrong stakeholder group
- Focusing on the 'what' rather than the 'how'

- Translating needs into requirements
- Stakeholders specifying unnecessary technical detail that confuses rather than clarifies the objectives
- Specifying ambiguous requirements
- Unrealistic trade-offs
- Ranking all requirements as high priority
- Determining completeness; establishing if there are any gaps or omissions
- Measuring the 'value' of requirements
- Inattention to business requirements

Requirements issues

- Incorrect requirements
- Ambiguous requirements
- Incomplete requirements
- Untestable requirements
- Shifting requirements

Human concerns

- Problems with natural language as medium
- Differing interpretations
- How do we know that the needs have been understood?
- Complexity of mapping real needs
- Poor understanding of the capabilities needed
- Communication difficulties
- Omitting 'obvious' information
- Identifying assumptions

Analyst issues

- Expertise not clearly defined and stated
- Need to access tacit and unknown facts and intuitions
- Analyst's ability to translate between user needs and systems requirements
- Limited user domain knowledge
- Complexity of integrating multiple perspectives and concerns
- Premature identification of solution/s
- Establishing priorities and trading-off needs and requirements
- Lack of appreciation of politics and power in the organisation

Not surprisingly, the majority of concerns appear to relate to softer factors associated with people, communication, understanding, politics, knowledge, needs, expectations, conflict, influence, agreement, disagreement and finding good people.

The seven deadly sins of stating requirements

Requirements involve people. Skilled specialists are utilised to work with different groups to identify their concerns and needs. The difficulties they address revolve around softer issues ranging from politics to biases, and from expectations to acceptance and collaboration. Yet, requirements also embody strategic considerations.

Needs analysis enables organisations to build a bridge between the strategic goals and the business case, on the one hand, and the design and deployment of solutions that underpin and support the organisation, on the other. The requirements management process meanwhile translates ideas and needs into a formal document which defines and delineates the expectations related to a project, product or outcome. Traceability provides a much-needed link between the levels and perspectives.

Project management is unlikely to succeed without the support of requirements management. Requirements describe how a project will meet the business needs that the organisation is endeavouring to address, as well as guiding the execution of that action. Without requirements management it is difficult to know what has been achieved and who might be satisfied with the results.

By way of a conclusion, the following list inspired by Meyer (1995) offers a reorganisation of the seven deadly sins in the context of requirements specifications.

Noise: The presence of elements containing information that is not relevant to the problem, or unnecessary repetition of the same item.

Silence: Relevant and important aspects of the problem that were omitted from the formulation.

Over-specification: Focusing on the implementation of a solution instead of the needs, or the problem.

Contradictions: Describing the same aspects in two or more different and incompatible ways.

Ambiguity: Use of language that allows the interpretation of a requirement in two or more ways.

Forward reference: Features are used before they are defined.

Wishful thinking: Using fanciful and unrealistic descriptions that cannot be met by a realistic solution or cannot be realistically tested.

Above all, the list seems to offer much-needed precision and focus to guide the exploration of our needs, and direct the execution of our desires.

References and further reading

Alexander, I. & Beus-Dukic, L. (2009). *Discovering requirements: How to specify products and services*. Chichester, UK: John Wiley.

Alexander I. & Stevens, R. (2002). *Writing better requirements*. Harlow, UK: Addison Wesley.

APM (2012). *APM body of knowledge* (6th ed.). High Wycombe, UK: Association for Project Management.

Blais, S. P. (2012). *Business analysis: Best practices for success*. Hoboken, NJ: John Wiley.

Brennan, K. (2009). *A guide to the business analysis body of knowledge*. Oakville, ONT: International Institute of Business Analysis.

Cadle, J. (2010). *Business analysis*. Chippenham, UK: British Informatics Society.

Cadle, J., Paul, D. & Turner P. (2010). *Business analysis techniques: 72 essential tools for success*. Chippenham, UK: British Informatics Society.

Carkenord, B. A. (2008). *Seven steps to mastering business analysis*. Fort Lauderdale, FL: J Ross Publishing.

Davis, A. M. (2005). *Just enough requirements management*. New York, NY: Dorset House Publishing.

Doran, G. T. (1981). There's a S.M.A.R.T. Way to write management goals and objectives. *Management Review, 70*(11), 35–36.

Forsberg, K., Mooz, H. and Cotterman, H. (2005). *Visualizing project management: Models and frameworks for mastering complex systems*. Hoboken, NJ: John Wiley.

Frame, J. D. (2003). *Managing projects in organizations*. San Francisco, CA: Jossey-Bass.

Gause, D. and Weinberg, G. (2011). *Exploring requirements: Quality before design*. New York: Dorset House Publishing.

Gottesdiener, H. (2002). *Requirements by collaboration: Workshops for defining needs*. Boston, MA: Addison Wesley.

Hall, G. (2002). Requirements management. In M. Stevens (Ed.), *Project management pathways*, High Wycombe, UK: Association for Project Management.

Hass, K. B. (2007). *Professionalizing business analysis: Breaking the cycle of challenged projects*. Vienna, VA: Management Concepts.

Hass, K. B. (2008). *The business analyst as strategist: Translating business strategies into valuable solutions*. Vienna, VA: Management Concepts.

Hass, K. B., Wesseles, D. & Brennan, K. (2007). *Getting it right: Business requirements analysis tools and techniques*. Vienna, VA: Management Concepts.

Hood, C., Wiedemann, S., Fichtinger, S. & Pautz, U. (2008). *Requirements management: The interface between requirements development and other systems engineering processes*. Heidelberg, Germany: Springer.

Hossenlopp, R. & Hass, K. B. (2007). *Unearthing business requirements: Elicitation tools and techniques*. Vienna, VA: Management Concepts.

Hull, E., Jackson, K. & Dick, J. (2011). *Requirements engineering*. London: Springer.

Jonasson, A. (2012). *Determining project requirements*. Boca Raton, FL: Auerbach Publications.

Meyer, B. (1985). On formalism in specification. *IEEE Software, 2*(1), 6–26.

Miller, R. E. (2009). *The quest for software requirements: Probing questions to bring nonfunctional requirements into focus; proven techniques to get the right stakeholder involvement*. Milwaukee, WI: MavenMark Books.

Pidd, M. (2004). *Systems modelling: Theory and practice*, Chichester: John Wiley.

Podeswa, H. (2009). *The business analyst's handbook*. Boston, MA: Delmar.

Robertson, S. & Robertson, J. (2004). *Requirements-led project management: Discovering David's slingshot*. Boston, MA: Addison-Wesley.

Robertson, S. & Robertson, J. (2012). *Mastering the requirements process: Getting requirements right*, Boston. MA: Addison-Wesley.

Sommerville, I. & Sawyer, P. (1997). *Requirements engineering: A good practice guide*. Chichester, UK: John Wiley.

Standish Group (2010). *The chaos report*. Yarmouth, MA: The Standish Group.

Stevens, R., Brook, P., Jackson, K. & Arnold, S. (1998). *Systems engineering: Coping with complexity*. Harlow: Addison-Wesley.

Young, R. R. (2006). *Project requirements: A guide to best practices*. Vienna, VA: Management Concepts.

4
Performance

HOMING IN ON PROJECT PERFORMANCE

Darren Dalcher

Performance measurement does not feature in the professional bodies of knowledge and appears to garner very limited attention in the myriad of textbooks and guides that describe and define the discipline of project management and the profession of project delivery.

While terms such as performance metrics, performance parameters, success measures, performance baselines and the status of deliverables appear in both the APM and Project Management Institute (PMI) bodies of knowledge, albeit primarily under the monitoring and control of on-going project activities, project performance management is not considered in an organised or integrated fashion in either.

Performance measurement is tasked with evaluating the value delivered by organisational activities, the impact on stakeholders and the effectiveness of organisational performance. Organisations manage the performance of results, activities, individuals, systems, products, processes, projects, teams, units, sections, departments and, indeed, the entire organisation.

Given the concern with the performance of projects, and the much-maligned poor track record of successful delivery, it is surprising that the interest in continuous improvement has not brought performance management into a sharper focus.

Measurement is ubiquitous

Our lives increasingly appear to be monitored and measured as data on every transaction, activity and interaction is recorded and stored. Every aspect of our being and every facet we engage with seem to be measured.

Universities record results, grades and credits. Political systems measure polls, attitudes, preferences, opinions and intentions. Credit cards monitor our spending habits, while shops observe spending trends and buying patterns. Financial systems feature currencies, investments, trends, budgets and accounts. We live by calendars and clocks that measure the passing of time; listen to weather forecasts that advise us about temperature, humidity and wind speed and direction; and take readings of our own temperature, pulse and blood pressure. Travel is paced by distances, locations and directions, allowing us to monitor fuel consumption and rates of progress. When we escape to the realm of sport, we find that performance is tightly controlled and measures of goals, touchdowns, rushes, wins, assists, passes, interceptions and even possession rates are religiously recorded and monitored to facilitate improvement and determine efficiency.

We live in an era that is characterised by the proliferation of measured data. As a society we generate in excess of 2.5 exabytes of data daily (exabyte is a term utilised to represent a quintillion bytes of data, that is, 18 zeros' worth). In real terms, the unprecedented flow of new data translates into 10 million Blu-ray discs stacked to the height of four Eiffel Towers, every single day; or to 250,000 Libraries of Congress filled with new data daily.

Yet, with so much data, we still strive for meaningful information that will discriminate significant facts that can guide our judgements. Indeed, improved performance requires not the deluge of data, but the injection of meaningful insights.

Making measuring part of managing

Chapter 2 featured the work of Fredrick Taylor and the impact it has had on management for over a decade. One of the attributed contributions of Taylor's ideas was the development of the process re-engineering community through the work of Michael Hammer and James Champy.

Michael Hammer, a US engineer and management author, is particularly acknowledged for driving and guiding the re-engineering revolution and developing the management theory of business process re-engineering. *Time* magazine recognised his contribution and named him as one of America's 25 most influential individuals, in its first such listing in 1996. In 2002 Forbes listed his book *Reengineering the Corporation: Manifesto for Business Revolution* among 'the three most important books of the previous 20 years'. The book has sold over 2.5 million copies, establishing business process re-engineering as a respected management discipline. Yet, today we return to one of his other books, *The Agenda: What Every Business Must Do to Dominate the Decade*, in order to refocus our interest in measuring performance.

The Agenda asserts that business conditions in the new millennium are likely to become challenging. Tough times will present as the new normal, where money is tight, competition is more intense and customers become even more demanding than ever. In order to compete in such a world, business must perform better than ever.

Hammer recognises that measurement is a key issue and an important management tool. Measures provide managers with valuable current information about performance, which can be used as a basis for effective and informed decision making that will in turn enable further improvement in performance.

However, he notes that organisations have not been able to harness the power of measurement (Hammer, 2001, p. 101):

> In the real world, however, a company's measurement systems typically deliver a blizzard of nearly meaningless data that quantifies practically everything in sight, no matter how unimportant; that is devoid of any particular rhyme or reason; that is so voluminous to be unusable; that is delivered so late to be virtually useless; and that then languishes in printouts and briefing books, without being put to any significant purpose . . . In short, measurement is a mess.

A key reason for the mismatch, according to Hammer, is that measurement systems tend to feature financial reporting mechanisms and data (ibid., p. 103):

> Financial measures – profitability, return on investment, discounted cash flows, or any other of the technically complex measures used by financial engineers – tell you little if anything of what you need to know about your business.

> Managing using such figures, he contends, is the equivalent of driving whilst only looking in the rear-view mirror or managing a sports team using last season's win–loss record to determine key decisions (ibid., p. 103–4).

The second criticism of such systems is their fragmented and piecemeal developmental record, as they often reflect arbitrary attempts to address accidental shortcomings observed over time. Measures added by departmental heads are often ill considered and added without due consideration for the essential elements of what needs to be measured. Such additions often reflect a mismatched belief that measuring segments of employee performance and individual units can offer meaningful insights into the state of the overall organisation.

Hammer reasons that managers lose trust in their measurement systems and eschew their readings, favouring intuition. Alternatively, they obtain limited results that are not reflective of overall performance and cultivate partial performance metrics, observing and commenting on accidental readings. The solution, according to Hammer, is to recognise that 'measurement is in fact an essential part of managing, not of accounting' (ibid., p. 109).

Hammer's passionate writing reflects a bias for action, and a pining for a measurement system that uses measurement information to actually improve enterprise performance, instead of simply recording stored readings.

The difficulty is in reconciling the measures of individual performance (as pursued by Taylor), whilst recognising that enterprise outcomes, the only true measure of global performance, can be pursued only obliquely through informed continuous improvement. Measurement systems therefore need to connect the two rather disjointed areas of individual operating performance and enterprise achievement through multi-level models that make sense of productivity, performance and success.

Measuring project performance

Hammer's perspective points to the need for a more strategic framework for making sense of business needs and expectations and clarifying the specific enterprise context.

The contribution from Dr Alexia Nalewaik rises to the challenge introduced by Hammer, but attempts to make sense of the needs of a wider sector by focusing on the general performance of projects. As temporary endeavours, projects pose unique challenges in terms of measurement, performance improvement and organisational learning. The chapter draws on the book *Project Performance Review: Capturing the Value of Audit, Oversight, and Compliance for Project Success* by Alexia Nalewaik and Anthony Mills (2017), published by Routledge.

While there are currently multiple resources emphasising metrics, key performance indicators and dashboards that can be utilised in evaluating project performance, there is a dearth of systematic or methodological approaches for conducting performance reviews. Typical measures on offer tend to emphasise traditional performance criteria focused around time, cost and performance parameters. Moreover, formal audits often focus on accounting measures, expenditure figures or compliance issues, neglecting the actual performance and impact aspects of projects. In many ways, often mirroring the concerns raised by Hammer, current approaches to project audits and reviews are simply not fit for purpose.

Nalewaik rises to the challenge by offering a complete methodology for conducting meaningful project performance reviews which also comply with audit standards. Her work emphasises a flexible approach addressing what needs to be done on projects which encompasses performance gaps and stakeholder expectations. The framework offers a dual focus, progressing horizontally alongside the life cycle of the project, whilst employing a vertical perspective which embraces stakeholders and organisational expectations.

The work conveys recognition of the importance of governance and organisational learning and improvement in the management of projects. Importantly, it also encourages a scrutiny of inputs (resources), project results (outputs) and resulting impacts. The approach is both responsive and dynamic, thereby accommodating and emphasising the uniqueness of both the project and the organisation.

Making measurement meaningful

Nalewaik's contribution to the discipline is significant. The proposed framework is modular and adaptable, allowing the review scope to be fine-tuned to address the specific needs of the project and the organisation. It also makes it possible to direct the audit resources to the specific areas that would benefit the most from the investment in attention, scrutiny and detailed review. It is particularly encouraging to see such flexibility in a discipline that can so often become characterised by normative and prescriptive adherence to methods, steps, recipes and the occasional dogma.

Nalewaik recognises that static (review) models offer limited value in a project world that is steeped in uncertainty and change. Her thinking reflects Hammer's chief concerns regarding the obsession with accounting measures and gazing backwards instead of looking forwards. Moreover, by providing a flexible and configurable approach to reviewing progress, she enables requisite tailoring, prioritisation and focus according to the context and prevailing needs within the organisation and the project. This has a triple impact of facilitating learning, correcting identified issues and enabling performance improvement.

Andy Grove, CEO of Intel, observed that 'there is at least one point in the history of any company when you have to change dramatically to rise to the next level of performance. Miss that moment – and you start to decline.'

Selecting proper measures and applying flexible review and audit frameworks can play a key part in identifying performance levels, current progress and future impact. By devising informed measures that address wider enterprise targets and achievements, alongside the meaningful measurements of individual efforts, projects and portfolios, we can seek to invoke the improvement, growth and development needed to sustain the project and the wider organisation. We can also try to ensure that we do not miss the point in history that requires informed change. Such practice can therefore become instrumental in identifying bumps, pitfalls and opportunities for adjustments and in securing an improved culture and appetite needed to sustain such progress.

US management writer and guru Tom Peters observed that 'excellent firms don't believe in excellence – only in constant improvement and constant change'.

Michael Porter reflected that the 'continuity of strategic direction and continuous improvement in how you do things' are consistent and mutually reinforcing. Ultimately, the role of performance measures and reviews is in actively and dynamically informing, guiding and directing that crucial journey to thrive, adapt and sustain excellence.

References

Hammer, M. (2001). *The agenda: What every business must do to dominate the decade*. London: Random House Business Books.

Hammer, M. & Champy, J. (1993). *Reengineering the corporation: A manifesto for business revolution*. New York: Harper Business.

Nalewaik, A. & Mills, A. (2017). *Project performance review: Capturing the value of audit, oversight, and compliance for project success*. Abingdon, UK: Routledge.

PROJECT PERFORMANCE AUDIT – A METHODOLOGY

Alexia Nalewaik

It all started on a normal workday, with two seemingly unrelated questions.

1   Why didn't this recent audit identify as many findings as the last one?
2   What can we do to win more audit work?

But they were related . . . and then, suddenly, I had a PhD topic.

Management consultants, by the nature of their business, live in a world where winning the work means survival of their firm, and improvements to their salary. Some will do whatever it takes to win the work. Others genuinely care about the service they provide. The two are not always mutually exclusive.

After analysing over 700 audit reports, the answers to the two questions were clear. Work was being won by other firms because they were able to price their services very low. However, in order to do so, they were reducing the scope of the audit to the bare minimum required by law. Their audit reports were, at most, three pages long – and that included the cover page and managing partner's affidavit. In contrast, a performance audit with broader scope could yield a report 30 to 100 pages long. Second question, answered. As for the first question, that turned out to be a combination of audit team skills and scope (Nalewaik, 2013). And yet, the answers to both questions turned out to be more.

Projects, especially construction projects, typically apply specialised project management techniques to mitigate the volatility, cost overruns, significant delays in completion and failures with which such projects are often associated. Audit represents one type of independent external oversight often utilised to provide an opinion on current project status and quality of management. However, variability in audit sampling and review techniques, team composition, scope, quality and availability of data, standards and other factors can impact on audit results. Unexpectedly, this research provided a contribution to two spheres: auditing and procurement. After answering the two initial questions, the research goal evolved to define key components in the execution of performance audits, in order to improve performance audit procurement and process, impacting on findings and thus their applicability and usefulness as a project and organisational performance improvement mechanism.

The objectives of project performance audit are to: 1) reduce risk; 2) enable transparency and accountability; and 3) create a culture of organisational maturity. Inherent in performance audit are the three concepts of economy, effectiveness and efficiency (Waring & Morgan, 2007). 'Economy' emphasises frugality and reasonability in the use of resources, 'efficiency' focuses on achieving results while minimising waste, and 'effectiveness' assesses the level of success in attaining the intended results. In evaluating the 'three es', project performance audit addresses the intersectional universe of resources (input), results (output) and impact. The research found that by significantly reducing the audit scope, certain performance audits did not deliver the depth and breadth of review promised or even implied. This, in turn, led to an expectations gap, wherein stakeholders had assumed that a 'performance audit' would truly evaluate stewardship and other concepts (such as equity, legality, fiscal prudence and rational/justified decision making), but the reduced audit scope did not really do so.

The research results found that different types and quantities of findings were generated by different audit scopes. Typical audit findings tended to focus on routine procedural, accounting and controls errors. On average, contract expenditure audits questioned 2.65 per cent of expenditures and performance audits of large complex programmes questioned only 0.04 per cent of expenditures. The majority (72.56 per cent) of the performance audits in the sample yielded no findings or questioned costs whatsoever. When more expenditures and project documents were reviewed, the audit yielded more qualitative findings. Including technical experts on the audit team increased both the percentage of expenditures questioned and the number of qualitative findings. Applying audit standards at first appeared to have a negative impact on the number of audit findings, but it was later determined that the reduced number of audit findings was related to limited audit scope and a lack of technical experts on the audit team. The research concluded that the two biggest factors that impacted on audit results were audit scope and the auditor's depth of project- and industry-specific expertise (Nalewaik, 2013).

Several years later, that research led to the development of a methodology for scoping and procuring performance audits. The predominant guidance available at the time was typically written by governmental audit offices, specifically for their projects, or by consultants eager to sell services; there existed no substantial guidance for the layman or practitioner. Books written on topic of project performance tended to focus on metrics and benchmarking. The performance audit profession currently has no academic or practitioner journal, no formal education, no certification programme and no official regulation. As such, approaches taken can vary widely and unpredictably, creating even more expectations gaps.

The Nalewaik-Mills Performance Review Method (Nalewaik & Mills, 2016) is designed to be a flexible, comprehensive and modular approach that may be applied to complex, multifaceted or phased activities, projects and programmes; to both private and public sectors; in construction; in non-construction industries such as information technology and manufacturing; and in other endeavours such as major event planning, company launches and mega-activity implementations. It draws from best practices in a variety of fields: audit, governance, project controls, Total Cost Management (Technical Board, 2006), project management, risk management and quality assurance; indeed, it enables the inclusion of best practices from any relevant sources, employing critical questioning in a system of interdependent problems. It is designed to be responsive to project and stakeholder needs at every project milestone. The modules can be reviewed individually, combined and/or applied on an as-needed basis, in any order, at any time.

Developing the audit scope requires a discussion about the cost-benefit of each module, and prioritisation; by utilising a flexible and modular approach, appropriate audit scope can direct audit resources to project elements that can benefit the most from the review. Finally, the methodology can also be used to help an organisation mature by identifying controls gaps, recommending process improvements and streamlining processes, thus decreasing variability in management, increasing resource optimisation, improving the predictability of outcomes and reducing risk. It encourages an iterative review cycle, in order to capture process and behavioural improvement opportunities.

As for standards, those written for performance audits were often just an amendment of existing financial audit standards (Davis, 1980), which (in turn) provide guidelines for audit engagement management (Brown & Craft, 1980), not audit methods. The Nalewaik-Mills Performance Review Method is designed to be compatible with any required standards, especially the ISO (International Organization for Standardization) 19011 International Standard, Guidelines for Auditing Management Systems (ISO Copyright Office, 2011).

The method has been constructed as eight modules, which together cover the breadth of key project inputs, outputs, controls and influences. The modules can each be included or not included, as appropriate for the specific phase of the project and the needs of the organisation. When subsequent audits are conducted, additional modules may be added, previously reviewed modules may be skipped, some modules may be revisited and all previous audit findings should be reviewed. When applied singly or combined, the modules target the audit work to optimise findings and continuous improvement, without constraining the auditor's discretion in approach. Figure 4.1 (Nalewaik & Mills, 2016) shows both the modules and their applicability at different times during the project life cycle.

Very briefly:

- It can be said that the success or failure of the project begins while it is still the idea that is being formed. Module 1 – Planning addresses this phase of the project, focusing on the steps taken to create the project, matching project

Nalewaik-Mills Performance Review Method

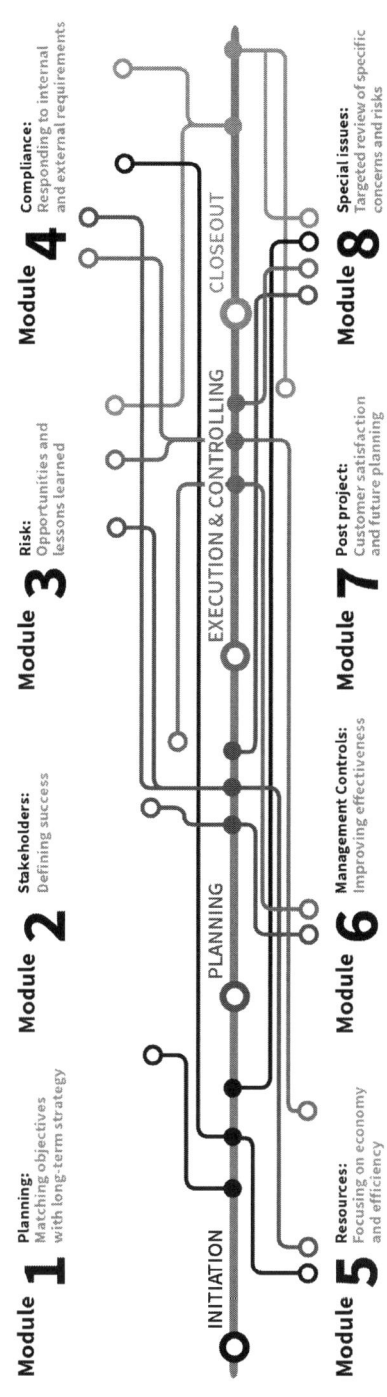

Module 1 Planning:
Matching objectives with long-term strategy

Module 2 Stakeholders:
Defining success

Module 3 Risk:
Opportunities and lessons learned

Module 4 Compliance:
Responding to internal and external requirements

Module 5 Resources:
Focusing on economy and efficiency

Module 6 Management Controls:
Improving effectiveness

Module 7 Post project:
Customer satisfaction and future planning

Module 8 Special issues:
Targeted review of specific concerns and risks

INITIATION

PLANNING

EXECUTION & CONTROLLING

CLOSEOUT

FIGURE 4.1 Nalewaik–Mills Performance Review Method

goals with organisational strategy and funding and determining how best to achieve those expectations (effectiveness) whilst satisfying economy and efficiency expectations.

- Key to expectations of success, failure, effectiveness and value are project stakeholders; success is a subjective concept, which can vary. Module 2 – Stakeholders considers the various stakeholders on the project, and their levels of interest, power, required input and influence. Identifying stakeholders also means understanding their concerns, motivations, depth of understanding of the project, tolerance for risk and likelihood to cause change.
- Risk, in the context of projects, is the chance or hazard of a loss, often commercial. Risk analysis identifies barriers to project performance, and opportunities to improve project performance. Module 3 – Risk focuses on understanding vulnerabilities, enabling the auditor to focus audit efforts, identify opportunities to strengthen controls and evaluate steps taken to mitigate known risks.
- Module 4 – Compliance. The compliance element of an audit is a review of the project team or organisation's adherence to processes, requirements, contract terms, laws and policies and procedures. Regulatory agencies, funding sources or corporate governance may require a compliance audit. Issues identified during compliance audit may result in recovery of funds, streamlining of processes and improvements to project and contract controls.
- The keywords of project audit (economy, efficiency and effectiveness), at their core, focus on the utilisation of resources as inputs. Resources to evaluate in Module 5 – Resources may include: money, time, materials, equipment, people and more; the concept can be broadened to anything that is consumed during the project.
- Module 6 – Management Controls focuses on controls processes, policies and procedures. This includes softer concepts in governance and project management, such as organisational culture, communication and reporting. The module focuses on improving controls mechanisms such that they are complete, optimised, reasonable, appropriate, consistent and provide value. Management controls, as defined in projects, include project controls, procurement, accounting, project management, IT systems and any other processes developed for the project.
- Project closeout, and the future of assets and deliverables produced by the project, are the focus of Module 7 – Post-Project. Much of what is reviewed is related to effectiveness, and the capture and future use of project data.
- Module 8 – Special Items exists as a placeholder for additional elements to review which have not been addressed in the other modules. This module is not intended to include elements that would typically be performed under a separate consulting engagement, such as: financial audit, inspector general investigations, formal risk modelling workshops, value engineering, claims analysis etc.

After applying the methodology on a number of real-world projects, it was codified further in a book: *Project Performance Review: Capturing the Value of Audit, Oversight, and Compliance for Project Success* (Nalewaik & Mills, 2016). The intent of the book is not so much to teach about audit as to help practitioners and client stakeholders to understand the factors that impact on performance audit results and effectiveness, so that they may appropriately define the performance audit scope, write the solicitation for services and select the appropriate audit team. In doing so, the book goes into some detail about areas of specific concern to project stakeholders (grouped as modules), how those concerns evolve during the project life cycle and why each module and concept is important to project success. As such, the book also serves as a handy desk reference for project management concepts.

In terms of the questions that prompted this trip down the rabbit hole, both are addressed by the methodology, although not in a simplistic manner. The method is intended to support continuous improvement by identifying actionable findings, thus addressing Question 1. Theoretically, it also increases audit effectiveness, as the number of audit findings has long been accepted as a measure of audit quality (Cashell, Aldhizer III & Eichmann, 1999). The answer to Question 2 isn't quite as easy. Creating the methodology and answering Question 1 also, in essence, created a niche market. Clients who commission an audit merely to satisfy audit requirements will still be inclined to limit the audit scope to the bare minimum and choose the cheapest audit proposal. However, clients and mature organisations who are committed to organisational improvement and transparency will be more inclined to appropriately broaden the audit scope and select an auditor with depth of experience in their industry. For those sophisticated project owners and stakeholders, the Nalewaik-Mills Performance Review Method applies. Use of the Nalewaik-Mills Performance Review Method is intended to support continuous improvement, a learning culture, increased organisational maturity, strengthened internal controls and project controls, transparency, accountability, stewardship and empowered critical questioning without retribution.

Note

1 In a landmark decision, the American Institute of Certified Public Accountants' (AICPA) Audit Standards Board has acknowledged that its auditing, attestation and consulting standards do not apply to the specific service of conducting a performance audit; as such, the standards are no longer required to be applied on performance audits (Audit Standards Board, 13–15 October 2015). While the present author does not claim direct responsibility for this result, she does note that she repeatedly beat the U.S. Government Accountability Office (GAO) over the head with her findings from 2011 to 2013, and the question was asked of the AICPA by the GAO in 2013. Coincidence?

References

Audit Standards Board. (2015). *ASB Meeting / October 13–15, 2015 / Agenda Item 3E / Q&A: Applicability of AICPA standards to performance audits*. Durham, NC: The American Institute of Certified Public Accountants (AICPA).

Brown, R. & Craft, R. (1980). Auditing and public administration: The unrealized partnership. *Public Administration Review, 40*(3), 259–265.

Cashell, J., Aldhizer III, G. & Eichmann, R. (1999, February). Construction contract auditing. *Internal Auditor.* Altamonte Springs, FL: The Institute of Internal Auditors.

Davis, D. F. (1980). Do you want a performance audit or a program evaluation? *Public Administration Review, 50*(1), 35–41.

ISO Copyright Office. (2011). *ISO 19011 – Guidelines for auditing management systems.* Geneva: International Standards Office.

Nalewaik, A. (2013, June). Factors affecting capital program performance audit findings. *International Journal of Managing Projects in Business, 6*(3), 615–623.

Nalewaik, A. & Mills, A. (2016). *Project performance review: Capturing the value of audit, oversight, and compliance for project success.* New York: Routledge.

Technical Board. (2006). *Total cost management framework.* Morgantown, WV: AACE International.

Waring, C. & Morgan, S. (2007). Public sector performance auditing in developing countries. In A. Shah (Ed.), *Public sector governance and accountability series: Performance accountability and combating corruption* (pp. 351–385). Washington, DC: The International Bank for Reconstruction and Development / The World Bank.

5

Anti-fragility

COMING TO TERMS WITH THE UNKNOWN: RE-INVOKING KNIGHTIAN UNCERTAINTY

Darren Dalcher

The topics of risk and uncertainty are often featured in the project management literature. Uncertainty is particularly prevalent: we grapple with uncertainty when dealing with the unknown; we acknowledge that we increasingly live in a volatile, uncertain, complex and ambiguous world replete with limited knowledge and uncertain and unpredictable patterns; we endeavour to acquire resilient traits that allow us to adapt and adjust; and generally, we seek more agile approaches in order to respond to a world that seems to change faster than we are able to adapt, or learn. Looking through recent contributions, one might almost observe that the obviation of uncertainty is an increasing obsession of the human race; yet, uncertainty itself, which appears to be an abundant feature of our creative landscape, is scarcely addressed explicitly in our recipes, prescriptions and bodies of knowledge.

While contemporary writings often assert that uncertainty is a growing feature of modern endeavours, particularly massive ones ranging from mega- and giga-projects to transformational societal change efforts, there is ample evidence that our ancestors also grappled with the doubt and paradox of uncertainty.

Scottish poet and lyricist Robert Burns wryly observed that 'there is no such uncertainty as a sure thing'. Prussian general and renowned military strategist Carl von Clausewitz noted that 'although our intellect always longs for clarity and certainty, our nature often finds uncertainty fascinating'. French mathematician and inventor Blaise Pascal commented that 'we sail within a vast sphere, ever drifting in uncertainty driven from end to end'.

English author and researcher Rupert Sheldrake pointed out that 'there's a certain kind of scepticism that can't bear uncertainty'. Indeed, the nature of the relationship with uncertainty was aptly captured by contemporary US scholar and public speaker Brene Brown, who recapped that 'I spent a lot of years trying to outrun or outsmart vulnerability by making things certain and definite, black and white, good and bad. My inability to lean into the discomfort of vulnerability limited the fullness of those important experiences that are wrought with uncertainty: Love, belonging, trust, joy, and creativity to name a few.'

Uncertainty thus encompasses a tentative balance between exposure, imperfection and vulnerability emerging from the unknown, weighed against a bias towards opportunity, progress, discovery and potential for improvement, development or growth that come in its wake.

US theoretical physicist and researcher Richard P. Feynman captured the essence of the peculiar yet critical relationship with uncertainty: 'I think that when we know that we actually do live in uncertainty, then we ought to admit it; it is of great value to realize that we do not know the answers to different questions. This attitude of mind – this attitude of uncertainty – is vital to the scientist, and it is this attitude of mind which the student must first acquire.'

Revisiting uncertainty

Knowing and admitting uncertainty implies recognition of the features and distinctions of such a state. Moreover, the emergence of new writing focused on unlikely occurrences, 'black swan events', fragility and general preparedness for addressing and mitigating the impact of the unknown merits a reconsideration of some of the more established but often neglected sources in risk and uncertainty.

One of the early detailed sources on risk is provided by the work of US economist Frank Knight (1885–1972), made familiar through his timeless classic bestselling book, *Risk, Uncertainty and Profit*. The book, published in 1921, is based on his doctoral dissertation at Cornell University and has been selected by scholars as being culturally important, and is now recognised as part of the classical knowledge base of civilisation.

Knight's book represents a very early, organised attempt to make sense of the distinctions between risk and uncertainty:

> Uncertainty must be taken in a sense radically distinct from the familiar notion of Risk, from which it has never been properly separated . . . The essential fact is that 'risk' means in some cases a quantity susceptible of measurement, while at other times it is something distinctly not of this character; and there are far-reaching and crucial differences in the bearings of the phenomena depending on which of the two is really present and operating . . . It will appear that a measurable uncertainty, or 'risk' proper, as we shall use the term, is so far different from an unmeasurable one that it is not in effect an uncertainty at all.
>
> (Knight, 1921, pp. 19–20)

In Knight's formulation, risk is taken as a measurable quantity, whilst uncertainty is regarded as true uncertainty 'of the non quantitative type'. Risky situations occur where the outcomes are unknown but are governed by probability distributions that are known at the outset (in other words, while we do not know which outcome will prevail, we can measure or determine the odds). Under such conditions agents endeavour to maximise economic gains through expected utility.

In uncertain setups, in contrast, both the outcomes and the probability models that govern them are unknown; so that we cannot know all the information needed to determine the odds. This is referred to as *Knightian uncertainty* or 'true uncertainty', as opposed to 'measurable risk', reflecting the general lack of knowledge, insight, rules, rationalisations or distributions that can account for potential behaviours. This position appears to chime with the view of information theorists, including US mathematician Claude Shannon, who observed that: 'Information is the resolution of uncertainty.'

Knight concluded that, given its nature, uncertainty thus gives rise to potential economic gains and profit.

Uncertain distinctions

To fully understand Knight's position it is useful to consider the philosophical distinctions employed throughout his writing. Knight makes a clear distinction between mechanistic thinking with static features and machine-like entities, and organic or biological entities characterised by change, processual development and adaptation. Perfect knowledge in mechanistic systems and domains is thus contrasted with imperfection in organic systems.

Knight maintains that uncertainty arises out of agents' partial knowledge about the potential outcomes and their implications (i.e. the exhaustive classification of all potential states).

> The essence of the situation is action according to opinion, of greater or less foundation and value, neither entire ignorance nor complete and perfect information, but partial knowledge.
>
> (Knight, 1921, p. 199)

Understanding of the potential outcomes is crucial to determining the presence of uncertainty. When talking about uncertainty Knight utilises the concept of 'an estimate of an estimate', requiring two separate and distinct exercises of judgement: 'the formation of an estimate and the estimation of its value' (Ibid., p. 227).

This is illustrated through his example which addresses the two sets of judgemental steps required:

> A manufacturer is considering the advisability of making a large commitment in increasing the capacity of his works. He 'figures' more or less on the proposition, taking account as well as possible of the various factors more or less susceptible of measurement, but the final result is an 'estimate' of the probable outcome of any proposed course of action.
>
> (Ibid., p. 226).

The first step is concerned with gaining an intuitive understanding of potential outcomes and states, whilst the second is concerned with determining the ability to quantify or qualify the different states and their relative merit and desirability.

It is therefore the presence, or absence, of uncertainty that determines the actions, possibilities and responses as behaviour conforms to the type of situation faced:

> With uncertainty absent, man's energies are devoted altogether to doing things; it is doubtful whether intelligence itself would exist in such a situation; in a world so built that perfect knowledge was theoretically possible, it seems likely that all organic readjustments would become mechanical, all organisms automata. With uncertainty present, doing things, the actual execution of activity, becomes in a real sense a secondary part of life; the primary problem or function is deciding what to do and how to do it.
>
> (Ibid., p. 268)

Organising for uncertainty

The presence or absence of uncertainty plays a crucial part in shaping the processes and structures employed in the pursuit of action. In the absence of uncertainty, organisations can pursue mechanistic structures focused on efficient execution, utilising a machine metaphor concerned with fine-tuning and improved efficiency. Planning and organising would thus endeavour to optimise results and reduce inefficiencies and waste.

However, the presence of Knightian uncertainty makes judgement and decision making critical to adaptation, improvement and survival in the organic or biological sense as advocated by Knight – which may also imply a financial survival imperative in a modern business context. Such environments reflect many of our experiences of new and innovative project and programme contexts replete with change and uncertainty that need to be addressed, where the delivery of expected benefits and meaningful value determine the perceived success and long-term perception of the undertaking.

So, where do we look beyond traditional risk management to secure the capability to deal with the unknown and the unexpected? Part of the answer is provided by the author of this chapter, Professor Tony Bendell, who questions whether our projects are fragile, robust or, indeed, anti-fragile. The chapter is derived from Bendell's book *Building anti-Fragile organisations: Risk, Opportunity and Governance in a Turbulent World*, published by Routledge.

Bendell has built up an expertise in developing anti-fragile organisations and structures. Anti-fragility offers an alternative way to addressing risk, by fostering resilience that benefits from disturbances and fluctuations. The approach appears to chime with Knight's interest in organic or biological systems, offering a mechanism for thriving under conditions of uncertainty. Indeed, anti-fragile organisations and structures are able to grow and strengthen over time, offering an alternative paradigm for dealing with uncertainty, governance and organisation.

Bendell (2014) employs a Darwinist perspective to immunise and strengthen organisations, systems and services developed as anti-fragile capability. Anti-fragile corporations and products are better able to survive the unexpected and thrive from the unknown, facilitating sustained survival in unpredictable and change-ridden environments.

Dealing with the unknown

Human society has long obsessed about avoiding the unknown and eschewing the uncertain.

Canadian philosopher of science Ian Hacking lamented that 'every moral teacher or spiritual adviser gives injunctions about how to live wisely and well. But life is so complicated and full of uncertainty that rules seldom tell us quite what to do.'

Yet, many critical endeavours depend on the ability to survive and thrive under such conditions. Indeed, for Polish mathematician Jacob Bronowski 'knowledge is an unending adventure at the edge of uncertainty'.

Consequently, the search for secure recipes and procedures works only in limited environments and contexts.

Reinterpreting Knight's distinctions in our modern terms would recall the need to distinguish between the known unknowns and the unknown unknowns and apply appropriate methods and frameworks that enable organisations and individuals to thrive under the relevant conditions.

Resilient systems thinking, emphasising adaptive, biological or organic metaphor and ways of thinking carries a promising potential. It can be viewed as akin to personal hygiene or sanitation; a way of improving human condition and enabling further growth and achievement over a protracted future, whilst facing challenges and threats.

The value of recognising uncertainty and embracing anti-fragility is in developing the mechanisms and capabilities needed to thrive and prosper. Indeed, Richard Feynman observed that 'it is in the admission of ignorance and the admission of uncertainty that there is a hope for the continuous motion of human beings in some direction that doesn't get confined, permanently blocked, as it has so many times before in various periods in the history of man.'

While achievement, development and growth often depend on embracing uncertainty, selecting the right approaches is situated and contextual. British philosopher Julian Baggini none the less sounds a much-needed note of caution: 'The mark of a mature, psychologically healthy mind is indeed the ability to live with uncertainty and ambiguity, but only as much as there really is. Uncertainty is no virtue when the facts are clear, and ambiguity is mere obfuscation when more precise terms are applicable.'

Ultimately, coming to terms with the unknown requires embracing the distinctions between risk and Knightian uncertainty; balancing anticipation and resilience strategies as needed; and adopting requisite resilience, flexibility, diversity and anti-fragility measures in order to thrive and prosper in situations of volatility, turbulence, uncertainty and ambiguity.

References

Bendell, T. (2014). *Building anti-fragile organisations: Risk, opportunity and governance in a turbulent world*. Farnham: Gower.

Knight, F. H. (1921). *Risk, uncertainty, and profit*. Boston, MA: Hart, Schaffner & Marx; Houghton Mifflin Company.

ARE PROJECTS AND PROJECT MANAGERS FRAGILE, ROBUST OR ANTI-FRAGILE?

Tony Bendell

It may be said that we live in depressing times. Our media is full of failing and failed organisations. From financial crises to the British Broadcasting Corporation, from the US Internal Revenue Service or the Veterans Health Administration to the UK Parliament, all around us is the evidence that our systems and safeguards are failing to protect their stakeholders from the slings and arrows of outrageous management and an ever more demanding and volatile environment. Clearly, modern life has an enormous dependence on the integrity of human systems.

But what of projects? Are they more or less liable to failure? Is our project management any better than our operations management? Of course, projects also fail all too frequently to deliver on time, to cost and to requirement. This is true whether we consider the catalogue of catastrophe in development projects around the world, including boreholes and wells in Africa, the De Havilland Comet, the Swedish navy's new flagship that sank on its maiden voyage, failure of government projects such as the UK's Department for Transport Shared Services Centre, or IT projects such as the early IBM Stretch supercomputer project. Project failure is not new and, it can be argued, not adequately safeguarded against, even today.

In a sense, it's all about how we manage and deal with risk

However, 'risk' is itself a human construct; our way of coping with, and trying to predict and manage, the unknown. It reflects the fact that 'Organisations of any kind face internal and external factors and influences that make it uncertain whether, when and the extent to which they will achieve or exceed their objectives' (ISO 31000:2009). 'Risk' is then defined as the effect that this uncertainty has on the organisation's objectives. This view of risk as a human construct is valid, whether or not one believes in a probabilistic or a deterministic universe, and applies as much in project management to achieving project objectives, as it does in operations.

The key issue for both operations management and project management is that looking at risk as we do in this way is not completely helpful, particularly in a complex, turbulent world in which there is an apparently increasing incidence of so-called 'black swans'. These are those low-probability, unpredictable events with major consequences. In my book *Building Anti-Fragile Organisations: Risk, Opportunity and Governance in a Turbulent World* (2014) I argued that, despite good intents, much of risk analysis and management as we know it today is part of the problem, not of the solution. My argument is that the way we conceive and approach risk and its management has led to increased exposure and fragility.

The core of this argument is based on application of the anti-fragility concepts of Nassim Taleb, the author of *The Black Swan*, who has been extensively lauded for his insights into banking and economic crisis of 2007–8. There is no doubt that whilst Taleb is a professor of finance, much of his arguments about risk, and in particular his emerging view of anti-fragility, apply also in other domains, such as companies, healthcare systems and organisational design and management, as well as, indeed, to projects of all types.

Fragile, robust and anti-fragile projects

Organisations, systems and projects may be fragile, robust or anti-fragile.

- Fragile refers to systems, organisations and projects that can be easily damaged, in terms of meeting their objectives, by changes or shocks in the external or internal environment.
- Robust refers to systems, organisations and projects that are able to withstand such adverse conditions.
- Anti-fragile refers to systems, organisations and projects that, like biological systems, are more than just robust and can keep functioning and, within limits, actually improve their resilience and performance through being stressed.

Anti-fragility is a new way of thinking about mitigating risk. With this view, to find out about risk avoidance, mitigation and management in human systems or projects we focus on the analogous characteristics of biological systems that, being more than just robust, *actually improve their resilience through being stressed*. Wouldn't we like that to be true about our projects also?

Applying this concept to the planning, deployment and management of projects of all types allows us to identify the characteristics of these that will not only mitigate against the realisation of hazards but also enable growth in protection over time. At the project level, anti-fragility (or not) is defined by the project strategy, structure and systems, its people, relationships and the culture of the project team.

Typically, some sources of anti-fragility in projects are:

- learning and experience
- real-time awareness of environment and internal project circumstances
- effective information systems
- the ability to take decisions and act quickly and well
- flexibility and agility
- good decision making
- shared and spread risk.

Of course, there can be a danger of applying 'one dimensional' anti-fragility, where we just rely on a single aspect, such as experience, and hope for the best. Often a practical approach to retaining anti-fragility in a project approach is to incorporate the development of the appropriate collaborative culture and multi-skilling; i.e. an emphasis on people. In contrast, technology solutions, such as 'hard-wiring' conveyor systems or reliance on restrictive standardised business software systems, are by definition inflexible, and are typically fragile.

Applications of quality management systems and ISO 9001, are inherently anti-fragile features within projects. In fact, all organisational and system information gathering and feedback loops that potentially use current performance as the basis for control and/or change represent anti-fragility features. This includes Strategy Review; Risk Management; Budgetary Control; Internal and external audit; quality control; quality assurance; developmental and evaluative performance appraisals; Health and Safety Executive assurance; continuous improvement, Kaizan, Six Sigma, lean improvement, agile deployment, and organisational assessment against the European Foundation for Quality Management excellence model (EFQM, 2018).

But there is a big 'BUT'. The ways that these systems are implemented are themselves typically fragile, rather than anti-fragile. They are typically formalised, delegated to middle management, routinised and automated. Their information base is typically inadequate and untimely. Decision making under threats lacks clarity, determination and learning.

Such safeguarding systems are typically also designed for robustness rather than anti-fragility, which also often implies rigidity. They have incomplete information flow and assume some stability and no 'black swans'. Even worse, there is a danger of their becoming compliance-driven rituals, with incomplete information, with most importance being given to the integrity of the paper trail for auditing purposes, and of their being given inadequate senior management attention.

In fact, there is a lack of a holistic approach to fragility minimisation and management in current practice in project and system design and execution. Thus, a key part of the anti-fragile mechanism in all these cases is the human role. And whilst risk management and quality management are anti-fragility features of our project execution, they are themselves often implemented in a fragile way. We can call this 'second level fragility', and it's a serious problem.

A basic fragility test for your projects

Many of my clients have found the following ten-point questionnaire a simple starting point for reducing project fragility. It is really a self-realisation tool, designed to identify where the most major dangers of fragility may be lurking.

You might like to try it. For each question, give an answer as a score between 0 (very bad) and 10 (excellent).

1   How good is our current project planning and management approach?
2   Do we include deliberate diversity of approach and deployment?
   - Diversity supports anti-fragility, as not everything is then likely to fail together. So, 0 = very standardised, no diversity; and 10 = highly diverse approaches.
3   How aware are we of our environment?
4   Do we learn?
5   Do we implement what we learn?
6   Do we learn and implement the learning fast enough?
7   Do we have the infrastructure to learn and implement learning?
8   Do we evolve, or are we essentially unchanging?
   - Again, evolution supports anti-fragility, so that 10 = high evolution over time.
9   Do we have the infrastructure to evolve?
10 How optimised are our processes?
   - Highly optimised processes tend to be fragile, as they are heavily loaded and stressed, and there is no space to intervene and maintain them if things go wrong. So, score 0 = highly optimised processes.

Ten common pitfalls of fragile project management

Arguably, globally our organisations and systems are failing with increasing frequency and magnitude, and the risk and quality professions appear to be ignoring it. The same may be true with projects.

In my experience, there are ten common pitfalls of fragile organisations, that I believe also apply to project managers and their projects. These are:

1   not knowing that they are fragile
2   not being joined up
3   knowing, not doing
4   doing risk management incorrectly
5   too much emphasis on money and short-termism
6   bureaucracy and emphasis on control
7   badly managing change
8   weak processes or an emphasis on initiatives
9   non-transparent decision making
10 naive offshoring and ignoring customers.

Ten ways you and your projects can become more anti-fragile

But, there are solutions. The key is awareness and learning, and applying what you learn. Unfortunately, this can often be a weakness in project management-based organisations, compared to functional management ones.

Suggestions to consider are the following.

1 Don't think you are there with anti-fragility. Realise that you never completely get there, but are also never completely not there.
2 Be aware, scan the external and internal environment, risks, scenarios and possible 'black swans'.
3 Be joined up and nimble, keep learning and apply the learning.
4 Avoid rigidity, ultra-efficiency and relying on robustness.
5 Don't automate, engage.
6 Reduce the fragility of anti-fragile systems.
7 Use diversity.
8 Apply precautionary principles; there are some risks you just should not take. Be aware of them, and stick to the principles.
9 Fail often and small. Experimenting on a small scale so as to learn is very useful. Experimenting on a large scale with your fingers crossed to meet the schedule, without having tried it small scale first, is potentially a disaster.
10 Stress test. Do not wait for something to fail. Check out the robustness of your project management in advance and learn how strong it is, and where it needs improvement.

Are projects and project managers fragile, robust or anti-fragile?

It might be argued that under commercial pressures it is easy to forget what project and risk management are really about. It's easy to dismiss the elephant in the room when you see yourself as only occupying a small part of the room, and it's not your room. The problem can be tackled. Anti-fragility gives us a coherent framework for unifying and utilising an impressive arsenal of already existing approaches and methods to take project management and risk management from the reactive to the proactive. But changing ourselves, our practice, is the hardest type of change.

References

EFQM. (2018), *The EFQM Excellence Model*. Brussels: European Foundation for Quality Management.
ISO 31000. (2009). *Risk management – Principles and guidelines*. Geneva, Switzerland: International Organization for Standardization.
ISO 9001. (2015). *Quality management systems*. Geneva, Switzerland: International Organization for Standardization.

6

Strategic initiatives

WE NEED TO TALK ABOUT STRATEGY

Darren Dalcher

Is there a link between project management excellence and long-term business or organisational success?

The traditional bodies of knowledge in project management have little to say about organisational strategy. This is somewhat surprising, given that the organisational appetite for projects is on the increase. Indeed, projects seem to consume an ever-expanding proportion of organisational resources, whilst anecdotal evidence points to a persistent yet unbridgeable gap between intention and execution.

The gap implies that while senior executives may be asking themselves if they are ever likely to see the value, or the benefits, implicitly promised through the organisation's project portfolio, project practitioners may be left adrift with little or no knowledge of the strategic preferences. Meanwhile, in agile implementations, local team autonomy may lead to execution drifting further and further apart from strategic intention.

The importance of strategic initiatives

Robert Kaplan and David Norton followed their pioneering work on balanced scorecards, strategy maps and strategy-focused organisations by zooming in on the need to link strategy to operations in order to develop and maintain a competitive advantage. Their book *The Execution Premium* (2008) focuses on the implementation of formal systems for the successful implementation of strategy. In the book, Kaplan and Norton describe the need to translate a strategy into strategic themes, objectives, measures and targets that represent *what* the organisation wants to accomplish. However, execution requires bridging the execution gap, and therefore strategic initiatives are utilised to represent the *how*.

> Strategic initiatives are the collections of finite durations discretionary projects and programs, outside the organization's day-to-day operational activities, that are designed to help the organisation achieve its targeted performance.
>
> (Kaplan & Norton, 2008, p. 103)

While the need for an explicit link between long-term strategy and immediate actions may appear obvious, they point out that their own survey reveals that 50 per cent of organisations fail to link strategy to short-term plans and budgets (ibid., p. 4).

> A senior executive summarized many executives' frustration with the lack of alignment between strategy and action plans when he said, 'half my initiatives achieve strategic goals. I just don't know which half.'
>
> (Ibid., p. 103)

Reading between the lines: So why do strategic initiatives fail?

Kaplan and Norton propose an initiative-management process model encompassing three distinct core activities required to align action with priorities.

1   Choose strategic initiatives: identify what action programmes are needed for executing the strategy.
2   Fund the strategy: identify a source of funding that is separated from the operational budget.
3   Establish accountability: determine who will lead the execution.

However, in reading the discourse related to the specific steps, it would appear that the true insights into the nature of the execution gap reside in the limitations and barriers associated with each of the steps.

Strategic plans require coordinated action that often extends beyond organisational boundaries, functions and business units. Kaplan and Norton reflect that in their original conception of scorecards they encouraged companies to select initiatives independently for each strategic objective. However, they subsequently concede that selecting initiatives independently ignores the integrated and cumulative impact of multiple related strategic initiatives (ibid., p. 104). Those following only the earlier writing of the two authors may thus miss out on the opportunity for integrating – choosing instead to optimise around individual activities and initiatives.

The new advice is that initiatives should not be selected in isolation, as the achievement of a strategic objective 'generally requires multiple and complementary initiatives from various parts of the organization. . . . We continue to recommend that each nonfinancial objective have at least one initiative to drive its achievement but also that the initiatives be bundled for each strategic theme and considered as an integrated portfolio' (ibid.; pp. 104–105).

In other words, in order to achieve the associated performance objectives of a strategic theme, it will often be required that the entire collection of initiatives, or the full portfolio of actions, is implemented. Successful execution with regard to organisational strategy thus requires a synergistic perspective rather than localised optimisation at an initiative or unit level.

Barriers to success

There are a number of additional barriers to the successful execution of strategic initiatives.

Integrated justification: Strategic initiatives may be justified on a stand-alone basis in different parts of the organisation, leading to strategic drift over the duration of the initiative.

Integrated funding: Cross-business portfolio funding is not common. However, the risk is that only parts of the initiative will be supported in different areas, leading to patchy or partial execution. Budgets typically focus on local accountability and responsibility centres or functional departments. However, strategic initiatives require uniform funding to secure delivery across the different business units and areas.

Integrated resources: A similar logic applies to the availability of people and project resources. To avoid local interpretation and prioritisation, strategic initiatives need to be resourced and justified centrally.

Integrated governance: Responsibility and accountability for the wider initiative need to rest with executive team members who can manage across teams, units and silos.

Strategic initiatives will often have a compelling business case that specifies the proposed benefits and the expected value proposition and these can be used as the basis for leading and delivering successful initiatives.

Delivering strategy through successful initiatives

Alan Brache and Sam Bodley-Scott (2006) refer to strategic initiatives as the 'means through which the vision is translated into practice' (p. 8). Successful initiatives thus provide the key to strategy implementation.

> At its simplest level, success is a function of two factors: the quality of the strategy that is guiding the organization and the effectiveness and efficiency of the implementation of that strategy.
>
> (Ibid., p. 15)

Changes in technology, customer demands, competition and social expectations often require drastic and fundamental responses. Previous chapters focused on the rising levels of uncertainty and ambiguity and the need for anti-fragility in many modern environments. To cope and maintain relevance in such contexts requires transformational changes to the strategic stance. Such transformation is often delivered, or attempted, through strategic initiatives. Yet, as pointed out earlier, there is a dearth of information regarding such initiatives and how to improve their track record of success.

To address this strategic deficiency, Dr Cooke-Davies considers the difficulties in delivering transformational change. His analysis identifies four influential 'strands of thinking' focused broadly around outcomes, people, complexity and leadership. Cooke-Davies explores major developments in each of the four areas before pulling them together to consider the major issues in managing strategic initiatives for success.

The challenge of strategic initiatives

US management professor and guru John P. Kotter reasoned that 'leaders establish the vision for the future and set the strategy for getting there'. However, there are many obstacles to delivering a strategy as planned, requiring constant improvements and adjustment.

The French general, leader and statesman, Charles de Gaulle, similarly reasoned that 'you have to be fast on your feet and adaptive or else a strategy is useless.'

Indeed, Michael Porter observed that there is a fundamental distinction between a strategy and the operational effectiveness that it engenders.

Aligning strategic themes with short-term project and programme initiatives requires periodic review of progress. Strategic-theme owners need oversight over the entire portfolio of action to ensure that all initiatives are progressing and the resulting actions deliver meaningful results.

British politician and prime minister Sir Winston Churchill wryly noted, 'However beautiful the strategy, you should occasionally look at the results.'

Delivering strategic initiatives, successfully, requires effective alignment, integration and active engagement across business units, strategic themes, interest groups and funding arrangements. It also implies understanding the role of change in the context of the wider business whilst making transformational progress visible across lines, units and boundaries. Yet, above all, perhaps it requires a deeper conversation about what it takes to implement and deliver in a strategic context, acknowledging, as Kaplan and Norton ultimately did, that initiatives can not be executed in isolated silos without looking at the wider implications. And that is why we really do need to talk about strategy.

References

Brache, A. P. & Bodley-Scott, S. (2006). *Implementation: How to transform strategic initiatives into blockbuster results.* New York: McGraw Hill Professional.

Kaplan, R. S. & Norton, D. P. (2008). *The execution premium: Linking strategy to operations for competitive advantage.* Boston, MA: Harvard Business Press.

MANAGING STRATEGIC INITIATIVES

Terry Cooke-Davies

Introduction

It is commonplace to hear the word 'strategy' used in conversations between executives, managers and staff when the topic of an organisation's intentions, aims and objectives are being discussed. Similarly, organisations' leaders are prone to launch 'initiatives' that are designed to change something about the business, to help implement its 'strategy'. Such 'strategic initiatives', therefore, are highly likely to consist of work that can best be viewed as projects, programmes or collections of projects and programmes.

An important study sponsored by the Project Management Institute as a part of its 2013 Thought Leadership series (Economist Intelligence Unit, 2013) reported that during the three years prior to publication, an average of just 56 per cent of strategic initiatives had been successful. The report defined a strategic initiative as 'a project, portfolio of projects, other discrete programme or series of actions undertaken to implement or continue the execution of a strategy, or that is otherwise essential for the successful implementation or execution of a strategy. This includes some – usually high priority – projects, but does not entail the entire project portfolio.'

Given how prominent a role projects and programmes play in such strategic initiatives, and the newspaper headlines that so frequently report on the failure of this or that major programme (especially if paid for out of taxpayers' funds), then this should come as a surprise to no one. There is considerable evidence from the field of projects and programmes to suggest that the low success rate is not particularly abnormal. Whether the data comes from the field of information technology projects, e.g. El Emam (2008), from major infrastructure projects, e.g. Flyvbjerg (2014) or from major organisational initiatives, e.g. Lovallo and Kahnemann (2003), all the results point to a higher rate of failure than might be expected, given the importance of projects and programmes.

It isn't as if the critical success factors for projects and programmes are not well documented – they have been extensively researched since the 1970s and are not controversial. Summaries can be found in many papers such as Fortune and White (2006) or Cooke-Davies (2004).

The trouble is that, like losing weight or giving up smoking, the principles are easy to grasp, but the behaviour (in this case organisational behaviour) is very hard to change. The more so because transformational change involves large numbers of people needing to do things differently.

Since the 1960s, however, management research and management 'gurus' have wrestled with the problem of bringing about transformational change and, in the course of this journey, have learned a lot about why it is so challenging. You could categorise the most important of these lessons into four key areas or 'strands of thinking'.

1   The first strand concerns what you could call the 'nuts and bolts' of good programme and project management: being clear about what you need to accomplish, knowing how well you are progressing towards those goals, and having the right means to make course corrections along the way.
2   The second concerns the people who are impacted in some way by the change. The past 20 or 30 years has seen tremendous advances in our understanding of what makes us humans tick, as fields such as cognitive neuroscience and psychology have started to gain insights from each other, and new fields such as behavioural economics have been developed.
3   Third, it is being recognised just how important it is to design programmes in different ways from projects, but incorporating projects and project management, while at the same time avoiding all forms of dysfunctional complexity. CEOs increasingly see complexity as a major challenge facing their organisations, yet they doubt that their organisations have the necessary capabilities to respond to it effectively.
4   Finally, there is a shift in dialogue away from 'managing' transformational programmes towards 'leading' them. An increasing emphasis is being placed on leadership and on talent management.

Each of these four strands of thinking has contributed important lessons that must be learned if strategic initiatives are to be delivered successfully, so it is worth summarising just what those lessons are.

Outcome, process and control

This first strand itself pulls together several different sets of insights and the research that underpins them.

Fundamental to all strategic initiatives is the question, 'What is it that you are trying to accomplish?' Indeed, during the 1980s the emphasis was all on this aspect of transformation. Business process re-engineering, for example, seemed to be very much the order of the day, particularly when the then newly developed practice of 'benchmarking' allowed Xerox to thrive in the face of intense competition from the Japanese photocopying manufacturers (Camp, 1989), or pointed to massive efficiency gains that could be made such as in Ford Motor Company's accounts receivable department, which employed 500 people, while Mazda's, admittedly dealing with only a half of the volume that Ford's did, had only five (Hammer, 1990).

But, in many cases, the focus on process re-engineering alone failed to deliver the results that it promised, and so we learned how important it was to start from the outcomes that needed to be achieved, rather than the activities needing to be changed or those needed to bring about the change (Schaffer & Thomson, 1992). The concept of 'key performance indicators' began to appear as measures of outcome, rather than as measures of improved activity.

Interestingly, the logical conclusion of this in the world of projects and programmes has still failed to be universally recognised, let alone widely practiced. Many organisations have not yet recognised how important it is to adopt a benefits realisation perspective (Crawford & Cooke-Davies, 2012), although there is increasing evidence of the influence of benefits realisation management in project and programme success (Serra & Kunc, 2015).

Project management, implemented poorly, can become a bureaucratic burden on an organisation. And all too easily, programme management can be seen as a way of imposing top-down control on project management (Maylor, Brady, Cooke-Davies, & Hodgson, 2006). What is needed is smart processes that are understood by all and that minimise misunderstandings between leadership, management and people doing the work (Sirkin, Keenan, & Jackson, 2005). Techniques such as Boston Consulting Group's 'DICE' and 'Rigor Testing' provide management with ways of testing that all is well, and that all remains on track, but, to be effective, the underpinning methods used to manage projects and programmes must also be simplified, and crucial checkpoints such as 'milestones' must be related to outcome measures of strategic value to the organisation, allowing the impact of changes to be assessed not simply in terms of the traditional cost, schedule and scope, but more significantly in terms of the value or benefit to the organisation.

Transparent control is the goal of such smart processes and value-related progress checkpoints, which is why different control tools are important for strategic initiatives. Programmes cannot be adequately controlled using just the tools of project management: there needs to be a programme structure that knits together the projects, copes with an increased level of uncertainty, and allows project managers to focus their efforts on the specific outputs and deliverables that their project needs to produce (Pellegrinelli, Murray-Webster, & Turner, 2015).

Strategic initiatives often impact on many different divisions, functions or regions within an organisation, and thus the controls and processes employed to manage and implement them need to be common to all the different units involved. That in turn calls for a framework of project and programme management that is consistent and coherent throughout the organisation, and aligned to the demands of its strategy (Cooke-Davies, Crawford, & Lechler, 2009). If these practices are not the norm in an organisation, then it is now understood that the process of introducing them is itself a significant programme of management innovation that needs to be approached as carefully as any other strategic initiative. There are many ways of approaching it, not all of which are successful (Thomas, Cicmil, & George, 2012).

Engagement of people

The second strand of thinking concerns the 'people' side of transformational change – perhaps the area that has seen the greatest strides, at least in our understanding, if not our practice, during the past ten years or so.

Perhaps the first thing to be said in this very broad field is that the leadership of strategic initiatives is not simply the responsibility of the programme managers who are tasked with responsibility for implementing the initiative. All too frequently, the cause of difficulties lies with the lack of intelligent involvement of senior executives, as highlighted in the Economist Intelligence Unit report (2013). However, this is a problem not restricted to strategic initiatives. Even from the humble viewpoint of project management there has been a growing recognition of the important role played by the executive sponsor (Crawford et al., 2008). Leadership of all such initiatives requires a partnership between senior executives and programme managers that allows their two very different perspectives to lead to balanced decisions on the basis of shared understanding – something that is easier to say than it is to achieve.

Coherent leadership, however, is only the first of the people-related challenges facing strategic initiatives. As a result of the failure of so many process re-engineering programmes in the 1980s, the 1990s saw an emphasis on the importance of 'engagement programmes' to win the 'hearts and minds' of those who need to change (Beer & Nohria, 2000), an insight that is backed up by current evidence, as shown in a recent report from the Project Management Institute (PMI, 2014). This is particularly important, given what we now know to be our human biases (Kahneman & Tversky, 2000), and the need for leaders of change to demonstrate high emotional intelligence (EQ).

Since the benefits of a strategic initiative are experienced not in the programme itself, but in the operations that use the programme's outputs, there is a growing recognition of the need to involve operational units in the benefits realisation process (Serra & Kunc, 2015), whilst at the same time avoiding placing too great a burden on them in the form of voluntary, unpaid overtime in the form of incremental effort to help the programme to deliver change to them (Sirkin et al., 2005).

An area in which there have been great strides during the twenty-first century has been the confluence of psychology, neuroscience and behavioural economics. The person who strides this field like a giant is Daniel Kahneman, a psychologist who in 2002 won the Nobel Prize for economics, for proving beyond doubt that people do not make economic choices rationally. The theory for which he was awarded the Nobel Prize is known as 'Prospect Theory' (Kahnemann & Tversky, 1979), and it shows that human beings are loss averse: we go to great lengths to avoid losing what we already have.

Building on this foundational work, our understanding of human biases has been widely investigated for the impact they have on our judgement, decision making and behaviour. Our apparent lack of rationality (Sutherland, 2009) underpins many of the behavioural challenges encountered in the management of strategic initiatives, and anyone wishing to explore the topic in greater depth could do no better than to read Daniel Kahneman's masterful and beautifully written book, *Thinking, Fast and Slow* (Kahnemann, 2011).

In his keynote address to the 2006 Project Management Institute research conference in Montreal, Professor Bent Flyvbjerg traced the link from Kahneman's work to his own work on *Megaprojects and Risk* (Flyvbjerg, Brunelius, & Rothengatter, 2003), which has become a classic. He also made the point that, left to their own devices, both the promoters of projects and the contractors who bid for the work conspire in a series of lies: the one because they want to believe that the project will be affordable, and the other in order to win the work. Specific examination of the costs of Olympic Games held since 1960 appears to provide compelling evidence to support this (Flyvbjerg & Stewart, 2012).

The impact of these human behaviours on complexity has been explored elsewhere (Cooke-Davies, 2011), and it is to complexity that our attention now turns.

Complexity

There are many different definitions of complexity, but none really does it justice. Almost by definition, complexity is beyond logical definition, which is why Terry Williams' description seems to me to be so apt, 'If you don't know what will happen when you kick it, then it is complex' (Williams, 2008).

Its worth distinguishing between complex and complicated. Something can be said to be complicated if it is composed of many interconnected and interrelated parts. Complexity, on the other hand, is related not only to the number of moving parts and how they relate to each other, but also to the predictability of each one, and thus the ability of the pieces to be melded together in ways that are foreseeable. Traditional project management tools, such as work breakdown structure, are excellent for complicated projects, but on their own are inadequate for complexity.

Complexity is also relative to what we know – at the boundary, our most ambitious efforts will always seem complex. Ancient building projects such as the Egyptian pyramids or Stonehenge must have seemed highly complex at the time, particularly with respect to the surrounding logistics, but they are very simple today in comparison with modern strategic initiatives such as the massively international programme to develop the Lockheed Martin F35 Lightning fighter aircraft.

Generally, it isn't technology that provides the greatest challenge in such complex programmes. A team at Cranfield University in the UK (Maylor, Turner, & Murray-Webster, 2013) have demonstrated the preponderance of problems caused either by what they call 'socio-political complexity' or by 'emergent complexity'. The first of these, socio-political complexity, refers not only to the behavioural challenges that were described in the previous section, but also to the cultural and political dynamics not only within the programme team itself, but also within the wider stakeholder communities. The second, emergent complexity, refers to the inherent uncertainty that arises from the intermixing of novel technological, human and social arrangements which give rise to unforeseen and unforeseeable consequences – what you might call the unknown and unknowable unknowns. Such phenomena are those that have been explored by the collection of scientific disciplines loosely known as 'complexity science' and explored in such works as Melanie Mitchell's *Complexity* (Mitchell, 2009).

A particular aspect of the socio-political complexity involved in many strategic initiatives is that they themselves are embedded within an organisation, like a cuckoo's egg in a nest, and the systems established to run the business often clash horribly with the systems in place to run the organisation.

Writing in *The McKinsey Quarterly*, Suzanne Heywood and her colleagues distinguish between two types of complexity – dubbed by them as 'institutional complexity' and 'individual complexity'. The former arises out of the strategic choices an organisation makes, the external context within which it operates and the management and operating systems that it employs to supply its products or services. The latter, on the other hand, refers to the ways that individuals operating within the organisation experience and deal with complexity – 'how hard it is for them to get things done' (Heywood, Spungin, & Turnbull, 2007).

As individual complexity rises, so employees find it harder to work efficiently and effectively, and both the individuals' and the organisation's performance suffers accordingly. When hard-pressed individuals are then expected to contribute to strategic initiatives on top of their already challenging 'day jobs', it is easy to see why this particular form of complexity provides so many challenges for strategic initiatives (Sirkin et al., 2005).

All this means that complexity has to be *navigated* (as the early navigators such as Vasco da Gama or Christopher Columbus did), rather than *managed*. And this calls for highly developed qualities of leadership at the head of strategic management – the fourth of our strands of thinking.

Leadership

The classic work on leading organisational change is from John Kotter (Kotter, 1995) of Harvard University. Maintaining that transformation is a process rather than an event, he argues that transformation efforts advance through a number of stages that build on each other. When managers are pressured for results too early, they skip stages and, as a consequence, fail. Having been around for more than 20 years, these stages are pretty familiar and have given rise to many imitations. Nevertheless, stages such as establish a sense of urgency, form a powerful guiding coalition, create a vision, communicate the vision, empower others to act on the vision, plan for and create short-term wins, consolidate improvements and produce more change and institutionalise new approaches still make sense in many strategic initiatives that involve transformational change.

Not all strategic initiatives, however, are only, or even mainly, about transformational change, even though many of them will include such elements. Under these circumstances, more general advice on leadership that is more broadly applicable is useful. Just such good advice grounded in extensive experience is provided by Ronald Heifetz (Heifetz & Laurie, 1997), who talks in terms of the *adaptive challenges* faced by people in organisations when confronted by the execution of new strategies (i.e. by strategic initiatives or their consequences) and the role of leaders in mobilising them to make the necessary behavioural changes.

Bringing this back more closely to the topic of programme management, the Project Management Institute introduced in 2013 (PMI, 2013) what it called 'The new triple constraint of project management skills' – technical project management, leadership, and strategic and business management. It has subsequently renamed these the 'Talent Triangle'. Surveys such as PMI (2013) place the weighting heavily on the leadership end. The general recognition is that the technical skills are the easiest to train, whereas the leadership skills are the most important and the hardest to train.

Pulling it all together: managing strategic initiatives for success

Each of the four strands of thinking that we have identified, points to a different imperative if strategic initiatives are to be successful:

- smart processes focused on the delivery of value that enable senior executives to provide strategic direction to empowered management;
- engaged people throughout the organisation working to implement the initiative in their own units, and aligned behind the initiative's purpose and concept;
- flexible navigation of inevitable complexity and avoidance of unnecessary dysfunctional complexity; and
- capable and knowledgeable leadership that delivers the first three imperatives.

Books, papers and articles abound about each of them. There is no shortage of good advice, or of evidence of the high cost of deficiencies.

Since this chapter is appearing in a book focused on project management, it should be emphasised once more that each of these four imperatives is *necessary* to manage strategic initiatives successfully, but even collectively they are *not sufficient* to guarantee success. They will deliver success only if the organisations involved in the strategic initiative have taken the time to develop those organisational capabilities that are essential prerequisites to good project, programme and portfolio management (Cooke-Davies, 2015).

However, strategic initiatives play an extremely important role in the world's economy. An article in *Harvard Business Review* described the problem: 'Since Michael Porter's seminal work in the 1980s we have had a clear and widely accepted definition of what strategy is – but we know a lot less about translating a strategy into results. Books and articles on strategy outnumber those on execution by an order of magnitude' (Sull & Spinosa, 2015).

Put that together with the alarming data already referred to from the Economist Intelligence Unit (Economist Intelligence Unit, 2013), from Boston Consulting Group (Keenan et al., 2013) and from the Project Management Institute (PMI, 2014), and the need to improve the management of strategic initiatives comes into a sharp focus.

References

Beer, M. & Nohria, N. (2000). Cracking the code of change. *Harvard Business Review*, *78*(3), 133–141.

Camp, R. C. (1989). *Benchmarking*. Milwaukee, WI: ASQC Quality Press.

Cooke-Davies, T. J. (2004). Project success. In P. W. G. Morris & J. K. Pinto (Eds), *The Wiley guide to managing projects* (pp. 99–122). Hoboken, NJ: J. Wiley & Sons.

Cooke-Davies, T. J. (2011). Human behaviour and complexity. In T. J. Cooke-Davies, L. H. Crawford, J. R. Patton, C. Stevens, & T. Williams (Eds), *Aspects of complexity: Managing projects in a complex world* (pp. 101–113). Newtown Square, PA: Project Management Institute.

Cooke-Davies, T. J. (2015). *Delivering strategy. What matters most, capability or maturity?* Paper presented at the PMI Global Congress EMEA, London.

Cooke-Davies, T. J., Crawford, L. H. & Lechler, T. G. (2009). Project management systems: Moving project management from an operational to a strategic discipline. *Project Management Journal*, *40*(1), 110–123.

Crawford, L. & Cooke-Davies, T. (2012). *Best industry outcomes*. Newtown Square, PA: Project Management Institute.

Crawford, L., Cooke-Davies, T., Hobbs, B., Labuschagne, L., Remington, K. & Chen, P. (2008). *Situational sponsorship: A guide to sponsorship of project and programs*. Philadelphia, PA: Project Management Institute.

Economist Intelligence Unit. (2013). *Why good strategies fail. Lessons for the C-suite*. Retrieved from https://www.pmi.org/-/media/pmi/documents/public/pdf/learning/thought-leadership/why-good-strategies-fail-report.pdf (4 May 2018).

El Emam, K. (2008). A replicated survey of IT software project failures. *Software, IEEE*, *25*(5), 84–90.

Flyvbjerg, B. (2014). What you should know about megaprojects and why: An overview. *Project Management Journal*, *45*(2), 6–19.

Flyvbjerg, B. & Stewart, A. (2012). *Olympic proportions: Cost and cost overrun at the Olympics 1960–2012*. Retrieved from https://www.sbs.ox.ac.uk/faculty-research/megaprojectmanagement/publications-0/working-papers-0/olympic-proportions-cost-and-cost-overrun-olympics-1960-2012 (4 May 2018).

Flyvbjerg, B., Brunelius, N. & Rothengatter, W. (2003). *Megaprojects and risk. An anatomy of ambition.* Cambridge, UK: Cambridge University Press.

Fortune, J. & White, D. (2006). Framing of project critical success factors by a systems model. *International Journal of Project Management, 24*(1), 53–65.

Hammer, M. (1990). Reengineering work: Don't automate, obliterate. *Harvard Business Review, 68*(4), 104–112.

Heifetz, R. A. & Laurie, D. L. (1997). The work of leadership. *Harvard Business Review, 75*, 124–134.

Heywood, S., Spungin, J. & Turnbull, D. (2007). Cracking the complexity code. *The McKinsey Quarterly, 2007/2*, 11.

Kahnemann, D. (2011). *Thinking, fast and slow.* New York: Farrar, Strauss and Giroux.

Kahnemann, D. & Tversky, A. (1979). Prospect theory: An analysis of decision under risk. *Econometrica, 47*(2), 30.

Kahneman, D. & Tversky, A. (2000). *Choices, values, and frames.* Cambridge, UK: Cambridge University Press.

Keenan, P., Bickford, J., Doust, A., Tankersley, J., Johnson, C., McCaffrey, J., . . . Shah, G. (2013). *Strategic initiative management. The PMO imperative.* Newtown Square, PA: Project Management Institute

Kotter, J. P. (1995). Leading change: Why transformation efforts fail. *Harvard Business Review* (March–April), p. 2.

Lovallo, D. & Kahnemann, D. (2003). Delusions of success. *Harvard Business Review, 81*(7), 8.

Maylor, H., Brady, T., Cooke-Davies, T. J. & Hodgson, D. (2006). From projectification to programmification. *International Journal of Project Management, 24*(8), 663–674.

Maylor, H., Turner, N. & Murray-Webster, R. (2013). How hard can it be? Actively managing the complexity of technology projects. *Research-Technology Management, 56*(4), 45-51. doi: 10.5437/08956308X5602125.

Mitchell, M. (2009). *Complexity – a guided tour.* New York: Oxford University Press Inc.

Pellegrinelli, S., Murray-Webster, R. & Turner, N. (2015). Facilitating organizational ambidexterity through the complementary use of projects and programs. *International Journal of Project Management, 33*(1), 153–164.

PMI. (2013). *PMI's Pulse of the Profession ® In-Depth Report: The Competitive Advantage of Effective Talent Management.* Newtown Square, PA: Project Management Institute.

PMI. (2014). *PMI's Pulse of the Profession ® In-Depth Report: Enabling Organizational Change through Strategic Initiatives.* Newtown Square, PA: Project Management Institute.

Schaffer, R. H. & Thomson, H. A. (1992). Successful change programs begin with results. *Harvard Business Review, 70*(1), 80–89.

Serra, C. E. M. & Kunc, M. (2015). Benefits realisation management and its influence on project success and on the execution of business strategies. *International Journal of Project Management, 33*(1), 53–66.

Sirkin, H. L., Keenan, P. & Jackson, A. (2005). The hard side of change management. *Harvard Business Review, 83*(10), 9.

Sull, D. & Spinosa, C. (2015). Why strategy execution unravels: And what to do about it. *Harvard Business Review, 93*(3), 58–66.

Sutherland, S. (2009). *Irrationality.* London: Pinter & Martin.

Thomas, J. L., Cicmil, S. & George, S. (2012). Learning from project management implementation by applying a management innovation lens. *Project Management Journal, 43*(6), 70–87.

7
Governance

IS IT TIME FOR 'GOOD ENOUGH' GOVERNANCE?

Darren Dalcher

The previous chapter featured strategic initiatives and their ability to connect strategy and execution. This chapter moves on to address the governance systems, structures and mechanisms required to implement projects and support organisational achievement.

The term 'governance' has been in wide use since the 1980s. It is often invoked in discussions around epidemics, risks, hazards, climate change, coastal erosion, environmental challenges, communities, globalisation and developing countries, but is neither clearly defined nor universally understood. The surge of interest in governance stems from the perceived limitations of traditional institutions and conventional structures, enabling a new social discourse focused on a fast-changing world where greater attention must be paid to people, practices, behaviours and activities.

> Governance refers, therefore, to all processes of governing, whether undertaken by government, market or network, whether over a family, tribe, formal or informal organization, or territory, and whether through laws, norms, power or language.
>
> (Bevir, 2012, p. 1)

The Oxford Dictionary defines governance as 'the action or manner of governing a state, organization, etc.'. Accordingly, the verb to govern is defined as: to 'conduct the policy, actions, and affairs of (a state, organization or people) with authority'. An additional explanation expands the focus, highlighting the need to 'control, influence or regulate (a person, action or course of events)'. The term governance, which first appears in Middle English, is said to derive from Old French *governer*, from Latin *gubernare* 'to steer, rule' and from Greek *kuberman* 'to steer'. The Cambridge Dictionary offers a more contemporary definition of governance, as 'the way that organizations or countries are managed at the highest level, and the systems for doing this'. The verb to govern is correspondingly explained as 'to control and direct the public business of a country, city, group of people, etc.'. Finally, the US Merriam-Webster Dictionary offers a more pragmatic definition of governance as 'the way that a city, company, etc., is controlled by the people who run it'. The underpinning verb to govern thus relies on the need 'to officially control and lead: to make decisions: or guide the actions'.

Governance can thus be reframed as a way of steering, organising, amplifying and constraining both power and actions. In other words, it is the way that the rules, guidelines, norms, practices and actions that underpin an area are developed, justified, sustained and regulated. Stoker further condenses governance to 'creating the conditions for ordered rule and collective action' (Stoker, 1998, p. 17).

Governance in projects and beyond

The sixth edition of the *APM Body of Knowledge* (APM, 2012) has been significantly reorganised around the concept of governance, which is the first key area introduced in the document. The discussion makes it clear that 'the governance of portfolios, programmes and projects is a necessary part of organisational governance' (ibid., p. 8), as it gives the organisation the required internal controls, whilst reassuring stakeholders that the money being spent is justified.

> Good governance is increasingly demanded by shareholders, government and regulators.
>
> (Ibid., p. 8)

The *APM Body of Knowledge* makes it clear that good governance includes the optimisation of investments, the avoidance of common reasons for failure and the motivation of staff through improved communication. The implication is that governance touches on many aspects including business cases, life cycle selection and utilisation, approval gates, decision making, communication, roles and responsibilities, performance targets, success criteria, sponsorships, stakeholder relationships and engagement, selection of personnel, deployment and handover sequencing, and organisational support.

Moreover, the *APM Body of Knowledge* further acknowledges that governance applies across many levels and areas:

> The context of a project, programme or portfolio is made up of two areas: governance and setting.
>
> (Ibid., p. 7)

> Governance deals with the procedural and cultural aspects that need to be in place to improve the frequency and level of delivery success.
>
> (Ibid.)

Such concerns further encompass the host organisation and its overarching strategy, the commercial nature of the work, the delivery partners and their relationships, the client organisations, compatibility with business as usual and the need to address change.

Governance, it would appear, can be defined and enacted at multiple levels, ranging from the international, globalised context, through the public, the corporate and the portfolio perspective, all the way to the programme and project levels.

Governance as a lens

The academic literature on governance is eclectic and relatively disjointed, reflecting a variety of theoretical roots (Jessop, 1995). Yet, despite the diversity of levels and plurality of theoretical concepts, the contribution of the governance perspective lies in its ability to provide a fresh starting point for reasoning about the changing processes of governing and the demands and expectations that they impose. Stoker (1998) thus views governance as a language and a frame of reference capable of yielding fresh insights and identifying underlying assumptions.

Stoker surfaces five key propositions (1998, p. 18), which are paraphrased and repositioned below.

1   **Complex network**: Governance extends beyond the set of institutions and structures that are drawn from government, reflecting the complex reality of contemporary decision making. This allows for the increased involvement of the private and voluntary sectors.
2   **Blurred boundaries**: Governance identifies the blurring of boundaries and responsibilities; it also recognises the mixing of social and economic issues and, more recently, the further addition of environmental, sustainable and ethical perspectives.
3   **Power dependence**: Governance acknowledges the power dependence involved in relationships between institutions involved in collective action and the potential for resulting unintended consequences.
4   **Autonomous networks**: The emergence of self-governing networks and partnerships places a greater emphasis on the need for the accountability of such arrangements.
5   **Enabler**: Governance is able to utilise new capabilities, tools and flexibility to steer, guide and deliver in increasingly demanding contexts.

Whilst governance has become a new focus for organisational discourse, the adoption of a fresh lens has resulted in the identification of new tensions and contradictions embedded within organisations.

The new paradoxes of governance

Many paradoxes in organisations revolve around the presence of contradictory and counter-productive tensions, such as the co-existence of authority and free will;

control and creativity; and discipline and empowerment. Such co-existence often requires new thinking to embrace the opposites perspectives, or contradictions, in a meaningful new way.

Governance offers an interesting perspective where, according to Müller (2009, p. 1), 'governance in organizations is a form of self regulation where the regulator is part of the system under regulation'.

An obvious question to follow is 'if governance is accountable itself, or whether there is a democratic deficit?'

Other contradictions that shed additional light on the distinct parameters and paradoxical implications of governance can also be identified as follows.

Paradox 1: Governance is the new control but is it devoid of power?

> In order to achieve greater control,
> Some times you need to let go . . .

The demise of traditional control forms based on precise rules and codified hierarchies is underscored by the need to engage with more complex, demanding and ambiguous contexts. Devising new control structures for such environments requires letting go of some of the prescriptive norms and replacing them with more dynamic, flexible and responsive forms. Governance can therefore create the conditions for an ordered and perhaps, even, a more responsive rule. Note, however, that responsibility without authority is meaningless. In order to carry governance responsibilities, the governance mechanism must be able to influence the organisation.

Paradox 2: Balancing control and collaboration

> In complex contexts, control can often only be achieved through shared responsibilities.

Responsibility is also linked to control. Control implies discipline and adherence to defined rules and procedures, leading to an aversion to risk and a distrust of variation. However, responsibility, control and influence also endow power, making a group or individual, and their particular perspective, important and influential in their views and actions.

Yet, the challenges of modern environments require organisations to respond in new ways and consider collaborations with other agencies and interests so as to achieve a common good. Such open approaches must rely on stewardship, where individual actors, often representing different organisations, are expected to behave collaboratively and cooperate in the service of the achievement of common goals.

As stewards, individuals may be trusted to behave in ways that are consistent with common goals and objectives. Shared responsibility thus enables groups to work together in order to deliver to the common good and become effective stewards of organisational resources and capability.

Paradox 3: Focus on shareholder value or stakeholder interests?

Corporate priorities versus getting everyone on board.

Powerful coalitions require a combination of interest groups that represent the priorities, needs and expectations of all critical participants. As organisations increasingly look beyond the financial aspects, participation by engaged stakeholders is increasingly sought to deliver meaningful results that will be used as intended in order to deliver actual value to the organisation. The governance philosophy can be located anywhere on the continuum between emphasising either stakeholder or shareholder aspects. Note that the value only arises from the actual utilisation of the assets or capabilities made possible by the project, and hence requires that stakeholders are ready and primed to play their part. A balanced approach between the two perspectives can therefore make sense and deliver workable and meaningful solutions.

Paradox 4: Internal diversity or external 'actorness'?

Biased insider knowledge versus impartial and broader perspective, with limited local understanding.

The strength of many boards and committees comes from the diversity of participants, especially those able to bring out to draw upon new sets of interests and perspectives. Identifying and agreeing on a common position may thus become subject to political negotiation, and committee machinations may drive consensus-building resolutions instead of local needs. Such boards rarely act as one, and negotiate in a more 'actor-like' fashion, which prioritises local issues. Consequently, the board may be deprived of both power and influence in important negotiations and trade-offs.

Paradox 5: Project governance or organisational success

Temporal projects versus overarching organisational priorities.

As we have seen, governance is addressed at multiple levels. The tension between short-term projects, which require governance structures and procedures, and long-term organisational priorities and needs remains a key concern. Decisions that may make sense at a project level, attempting to optimise local considerations, may make less sense from a portfolio or a corporate organisational perspective. Governance structures therefore need to identify the different levels of control and assurance that are being applied and to address decisions and concerns at the right level (which may vary between shaping strategy and influencing execution). Note that rapid change, adjustments and adaptation may further challenge the division between levels of governance and the various spheres of influence. Decision making and prioritisation may also be challenged to account for emerging conditions as local project concerns and wider organisational priorities may further diverge over time. This can also translate into an escalating inability of the board to turn bold ambition into meaningful change, due to limited implementation capability, or can simply manifest as a disconnect between strategic priorities and execution.

Establishing governance

Governance is sometimes referred to as the 'conduct of conduct'. What is often missing is advice and guidance regarding how to implement effective governance mechanisms.

This chapter by Martin Samphire acknowledges the need for developing governance capability and provides a detailed introduction to the governance landscape. Samphire identifies the key enablers, shares established guidelines and formulates a list of ten 'golden rules' required for successful governance. Sampire's contribution is in addressing many of the key concerns and in providing guidance to questions such as how much governance is enough. He also identifies the key players with the main lines of accountability and provides insights into embedding governance into the wider organisation, connecting it to the board and beginning the conversation about the success and failure of governance efforts. Crucially, his reflections on governance capture the different levels of perspectives around projects, programmes, portfolios; integrating them with business as usual and the corporate governance mechanisms.

Fink (2016) notes the distinction between *management*, which focuses on the current and internal aspect of the organisation, and *governance*, which is concerned with the dual demands of future and external requirements. The governance emphasis encourages an outcome-oriented view, emphasising effectiveness measured by business success, as opposed to zooming in on the efficiency of the execution effort. The broader scope resulting from a governance perspective thus replaces the immediate concerns of management with organisational leadership priorities tuned in to corporate targets and ambitions.

Directors looking to begin their journey towards the effective use of project management in their organisations can now benefit from two international standards that can be used as a starting point:

ISO/IEC 38500:2015 Information technology – Governance of IT for the organization,
provides a framework for the effective governance of IT to assist those at the
highest levels of organisations to understand and fulfil their legal, regulatory
and ethical obligations. The standard applies to the governance of the organisation's current and future use of IT, including management processes and
decisions. These processes can be controlled by IT specialists within the
organisation, external service providers or business units internal to the organisation and are applicable to organisations of all sizes, from the smallest to the
largest, regardless of the extent of their use of IT.

ISO 21505:2017 Project, programme and portfolio management – Guidance on governance,
describes the context of, and offers guidelines for the governance of projects,
programmes and portfolios. The standard can be used for assessment, assurance
or verification of the governance function for projects, programmes or portfolios. The document is intended to provide guidance for directors, sponsors,
steering committees, portfolio owners and the project management office, as
well as governing bodies, executives and senior managers who influence,
impact upon or make decisions regarding the governance of projects, programmes and portfolios.

Both standards define the governance of their respective disciplines as a subset
or domain of the wider-ranging organisational governance. Indeed, ISO 21505
describes it as 'the principles, policies and framework by which an organisation is
directed and controlled'. They also both share Fink's distinction between
management and governance, with the governing body setting the objectives and
rules for the organisation, thereby leaving management to achieve the objectives
whilst working within the 'rules'.

The international standards give governance the added credibility, recognition
and legitimacy needed to establish effective mechanisms of governance at the project, programme and portfolio management levels. The standards can then be
supported by more practical implementation guides, such as the guidelines put
forward by the UK's Association for Project Management.

Ultimate challenge: moving from total integrity to good enough governance

Evans (2012) introduces integrity in public administration as a metaphor for
accountable, transparent, competent and responsive governance underpinned by
the concept of public value. The integrity metaphor chimes with the observation
of US architect and system theorist Buckminster Fuller that 'integrity is the essence
of everything successful' and with Molière's credo that 'if everyone was clothed
with integrity, if every heart were just, frank, kindly, the other virtues would
be well-nigh useless'. It also matches the recorded aspiration of Indian prime
minister Narendra Modi, who elucidates that 'good governance with good

intentions is the hallmark of our government. Implementation with integrity is our core passion.'

Utilising integrity in the application of values, principles and norms offers the cornerstone of good governance. Evans (2012) consequently notes that the design of effective integrity requires an informed understanding of the obstacles to the achievement of integrity in public administration systems and a significant effort to implement measures to overcome them.

However, as we have already surmised, governing is an intricate challenge that requires a constant act of balancing of different roles, interests and perspectives to provide an organising viewpoint. Moreover, governance inevitably recognises the rising complexity and the need for multilevel governing that takes account of the intricacy, uncertainty and the various levels, expectations and needs. The application of effective governance, irrespective of parsimony, thus requires recognition of the variety and contingency of governance.

Grindle (2004) asserts that the delivery of a good governance agenda is unrealistically long and growing longer over time. Recognising the implausibility of good governance as a project of modernity, he instead makes a case for *good enough* governance. Grindle (2007) acknowledges the limit on resources, including money, time, knowledge and human and organisational capacities.

Good Enough Governance (Grindle, 2004; 2012) offers an alternative informed by:

- acceptance of the limitations of modern institutions;
- recognition that governance capabilities need to evolve over time;
- explicit acknowledgement that trade-offs and priorities cannot all be pursued at once; and,
- learning about what's working rather than focusing solely on governance gaps.

The idea of a *good enough* strategy or heuristic is common in a number of other domains, including decision making, problem solving, administrative behaviour and morality and ethics circles under circumstances in which an optimal solution cannot be determined or reached. Lack of information and inability to exhaustively explore or quantify all potential options may render the optimal unachievable. The notion of a good enough, or 'satisficing' solution, advocated by US Nobel laureate in economics Professor Herb Simon, offers an alternative and highly pragmatic approach to rationality. Such bounded rationality allows actors to limit the search for optimal solutions and stop when a good-enough alternative is reached. Moreover, it reduces the demand on the scarce resource of attention, limits the search period and enables participants to proceed with a workable, albeit less than perfect way forward.

> Evidently, organisms adapt well enough to 'satisfice'; they do not, in general, 'optimize.'
>
> (Simon, 1956, p. 129)

In an information-rich world, the wealth of information means a dearth of something else: a scarcity of whatever it is that information consumes. What information consumes is rather obvious: it consumes the attention of its recipients. Hence a wealth of information creates a poverty of attention and a need to allocate that attention efficiently among the overabundance of information sources that might consume it.

(Simon, 1971, pp. 40–41)

Grindle (2004; 2007) maintains that it is better therefore to assess feasibility more carefully; target fewer changes; and work towards *good enough* rather than ideal conditions of governance. Nonetheless, he detects a further paradox: the greater the need for improved governance, the more difficult it is likely to be to achieve *good enough governance*.

The answer is likely to be found in gradual deployment and development. The idea of *good enough governance* offers a limited but informed dynamic capability that can evolve and improve in an effort to provide integrated governance. Rather than be an end in itself, the target of good governance can become the product of intelligent application of *good enough governance* that is allowed to grow, mature and evolve. Indeed, in recognising the limitations of reality and postponing the search for matching perfection, we may already begin to establish the foundation for an informed and relevant version of the pertinent governance needed to assure the integrity of our present affairs against our future intentions.

References

APM. (2012). *APM Body of Knowledge* (6th ed.). Princes Risborough: Association of Project Management.

Bevir, M. (2012). *Governance: A very short Introduction*. Oxford: Oxford University Press.

Evans, M. (2012). Beyond the integrity paradox – towards 'good enough' governance? *Policy Studies*, *33*(1), 97–113.

Fink, D. (2016). *Project risk governance: Managing uncertainty and creating organisational value*. Abingdon: Routledge.

Grindle, M. S. (2004). Good enough governance: poverty reduction and reform in developing countries. *Governance*, *17*(4), 525–548.

Grindle, M. S. (2007). Good enough governance revisited. *Development Policy Review*, *25*(5), 533–574.

Grindle, M. (2012). Good governance: The inflation of an idea. *Planning ideas that matter*, 259–282.

Jessop, B. (1995). The regulation approach, governance and post-Fordism: Alternative perspectives on economic and political change? *Economy and society*, *24*(3), 307–333.

Müller, R. (2009). *Project governance (Fundamentals of project management)*. Farnham: Gower Publishing.

Simon, H. A. (1956). Rational choice and the structure of the environment. *Psychological Review*, *63*(2), 129–138.

Simon, H. A. (1971) Designing organizations for an information-rich world. In M. Greenberger (Ed.), *Computers, communication, and the public interest* (pp. 40–41). Baltimore, MD: The Johns Hopkins Press.

Stoker, G. (1998). Governance as theory: Five propositions. *International Social Science Journal, 50*(155), 17–28.

PROJECT GOVERNANCE

Martin Samphire

There is a strong correlation between good governance and more successful projects. Good governance is taking on a more prominent role in senior executives' minds as greater scrutiny is exercised and accountability for performance is expected. So what does good governance of project management look like and how can it be achieved? This chapter sets out some of the core principles, identifies the key players and enablers and provides ten golden rules of good governance.

Introduction

Project failure rates and the reasons for failure are little different now from 30 years ago. The UK Cabinet Office and National Audit Office (NAO) list common causes of failures that have been well publicised over the last ten years – which strongly resemble those identified by the Harvard Business School some 30 years previously:

- lack of clear link between the project and the organisation's key strategic priorities, including agreed measures of success;
- lack of clear senior management and ministerial ownership and leadership;
- lack of effective engagement with stakeholders;
- lack of skills and proven approach to project management and risk management;
- too little attention to breaking development and implementation into manageable steps;
- evaluation of proposals driven by initial price rather than long-term value for money (especially securing delivery of business benefits);
- lack of understanding of and contact with the supply industry at senior levels in the organisation.

All of the above are mainly poor governance issues. A recent survey by the UK's Association for Project Management (APM, 2015) confirmed that governance elements are key factors in project success. The Project Management Institute (PMI, 2014) Pulse of the Profession Survey and the PricewaterhouseCooper (PwC, 2012) Global Survey have indicated that there is a competitive advantage for businesses in developing good governance practice.

One cause of governance failure is that organisations become 'comatose' and do not always enforce learning from past mistakes and successes. Moreover, the project environment is becoming increasingly more dynamic, so organisations need to be more agile and flexible in their governance response. 'I've started so I'll finish' is no longer an appropriate strategy.

Why does governance matter?

Organisations invest at least 30 per cent of their turnover on projects (many spend much more). There is now a greater recognition that good governance of projects and corporate portfolios is core to success, and this is borne out by research. For example, 'Fit-for-purpose governance strongly influences project and programme success' (PwC, 2012) and 'higher performance is correlated with higher maturity' (ibid.). 'High performing organisations complete 89% of their projects, while low performers complete only 36% successfully' (PMI, 2014).

At times some members of senior teams neglect good governance until things go wrong. Boards (whether in the private or public sector) have a duty of care to shareholders and other stakeholders when investing in projects that will impact on their bottom line and reputation.

Governance needs to be a strategic focus for all organisations. The UK NAO Report (NAO, 2013) on the Universal Credit programme revealed a number of governance failures, including:

- overambitious timescales
- unclear implementation strategy
- lack of appropriate controls
- use of a novel (for the department) methodology
- lack of sponsor continuity.

Similarly, reviews of the failed franchise competition for the West Coast Mainline in 2012 (NAO, 2012) found a number of governance failings:

- unclear objectives
- poor sponsorship and continuity
- poor oversight
- lack of transparency
- poor planning
- unclear roles and responsibilities for approvals

- too much reliance on quality assurance reviews
- 'the departments' governance lacked efficacy'.

The governance landscape

The overriding aim of governance of project management is to ensure that an organisation achieves change successfully with confidence, transparency and control. It should ensure that the organisation is aware of risks, minimises project failures and maximises the beneficial outcomes (value) from its overall portfolio of projects in a sustainable and transparent manner.

The link between corporate governance and the governance of projects, programmes and portfolios (3P) and project, programme and portfolio management (3PM) is paramount. Most organisations have a governance hierarchy and landscape that can be simplified as shown in Figure 7.1. It is critical to differentiate projects (new or change) from 'not-projects' (business as usual) in any organisation because the required governance and management approaches are different (PwC, 2012).

Equally, it is important to differentiate the 'governance of project management' from the governance of individual projects or programmes and also to understand how these relate to the overall operations or 'business as usual' governance. Publications like the PMI's *Guide to the Body of Knowledge* (PMI, 2013), *Prince 2* (OGC, 2009) and *Managing Successful Programmes* (OGC, 2007) describe methods covering aspects of the governance of individual projects and programmes. The governance of project management is best described in publications such as the *APM Body of Knowledge* (APM, 2012) and particularly APM's *Directing Change* (APM, 2011).

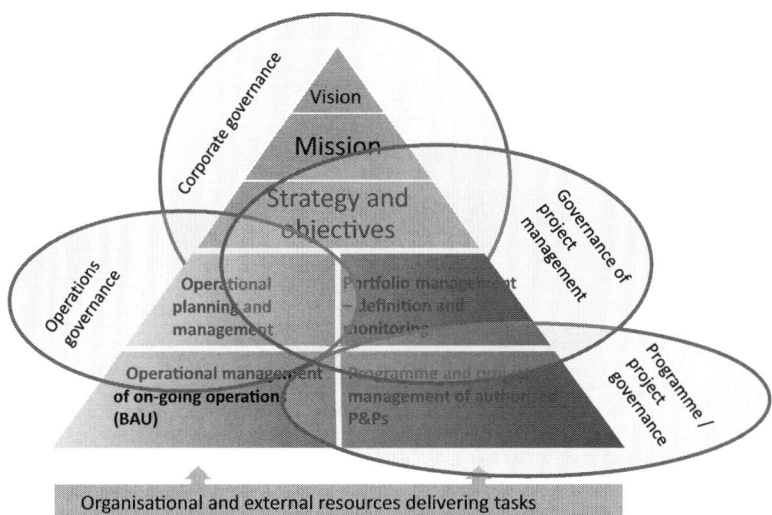

FIGURE 7.1 Generic Organisational Governance Linkages

OECD framework

The Organisation for Economic Co-operation and Development (OECD, 2004) lists the three main elements of a corporate governance framework:

1   A set of relationships between a company's management, its board, its shareholders and other stakeholders.
2   A structure through which the objectives of the company are set and the means of attaining those objectives and monitoring performance are determined.
3   Proper incentives for the board and management to pursue objectives that are in the interests of the company and its shareholders.

This governance framework is also relevant to project, programme and portfolio management.

The UK Corporate Governance Code

The UK Corporate Governance Code (FRC, 2012) states that 'governance is about what the board of a company does and how it sets the values of the company'. Good governance is about accountability, transparency, probity and focus on the sustainable success of an entity over the longer term.

One of the key roles for the board includes establishing the culture, values and ethics of the company. It is important that the board sets the correct 'tone from the top'. The directors should lead by example and ensure that good standards of behaviour permeate throughout all levels of the organisation. This will help to prevent misconduct and unethical practices and to support the delivery of long-term success. The 2014 update of the Code was designed to strengthen the focus of companies and investors on the longer term and the sustainability of value creation, and requires the provision by companies of information about the risks which affect longer-term viability. As such, there is addendum guidance to the Code specifically aimed at risk management, internal financial and business reporting. The *Corporate Governance Guidance and Principles for Unlisted Companies in the UK* (IoD, 2010) has a similar focus.

The crucial element of *The UK Corporate Governance Code* that impacts on the governance of project management is that the overall responsibility and accountability for good governance sits firmly with the board.

Governance of individual projects and programmes

Governance arrangements for individual projects and programmes are linked to the overall governance of project management primarily via the role of the project/programme sponsor, the corporate project management method, portfolio management and review and assurance bodies. Key success measures include:

- delivery of the project to time, cost and quality/performance criteria (the project manager measure);
- realisation of desired benefits (the sponsor measure).

Governance of project management

The governance of project management concerns those areas of corporate governance that are specifically related to project/change activities – across the whole enterprise. I would define it as:

> the set of policies, regulations, functions, culture, processes, procedures, relationships and responsibilities that define the establishment, management, control and reporting of projects, programmes and portfolio. Good project management governance sets the environment, boundaries, culture and regulatory framework for individual projects, programmes and the overall portfolio to succeed.

Governance of the portfolio includes choosing and prioritising projects to best meet strategic objectives. Stopping a project in the portfolio may be seen as a failure for the project sponsor and project manager, but a success for the overall business and portfolio manager – as long as it is done at the earliest opportunity. *Failing early is the new success*.

Established guidelines

We should all support the purpose of good governance, but what does 'good' look like and what do you need to put in place? Often, boards of directors want an instant 'already engineered' solution. However, as David Shannon, APM Governance Specific Interest Group chairman from 2003 to 2012, said 'governance is like nailing jelly to a wall'. Good governance in one organisation looks different from that in another.

Governance of project management principles

Good practice guidelines for governance exist and are well established – they have been developed over many years to address common causes of failure. The best of the published guidelines for governance of project management is contained in the APM publication *Directing Change* (APM, 2011), which states the following.

- The board has overall responsibility for the governance of project management.
- The organisation differentiates between projects and non-project-based activities.
- Roles and responsibilities for the governance of project management are defined clearly.

- Disciplined governance arrangements, supported by appropriate cultures, methods, resources and controls are applied throughout the project life cycle. Every project has a sponsor.
- There is a demonstrable coherent and supporting relationship between the project portfolio and the business strategy and policies, for example ethics and sustainability.
- All projects have an approved plan containing authorisation points at which the business case, inclusive of cost, benefits and risk is reviewed. Decisions made at authorisation points are recorded and communicated.
- Members of delegated authorisation bodies have sufficient representation, competence, authority and resources to enable them to make appropriate decisions.
- Project business cases are supported by relevant and realistic information that provides a reliable basis for making authorisation decisions.
- The board or its delegated agents decide when independent scrutiny of projects or project management systems is required, and implement such assurance accordingly.
- There are clearly defined criteria for reporting project status and for the escalation of risks and issues to the levels required by the organisation.
- The organisation fosters a culture of improvement and of frank internal disclosure of project management information.
- Project stakeholders are engaged at a level that is commensurate with their importance to the organisation and in a manner that fosters trust.
- Projects are closed when they are no longer justified as part of the organisation's portfolio.

Key enablers

Before we get to the ten golden rules for good governance, we need to look at the key underpinning enablers that allow an organisation to get started on the journey to better project management governance. Implementation of good governance principles is not easy. There are two essential enablers:

- the acceptance of a framework for project management in the organisation; and
- the crucial role of the board.

Framework

Organisations need to consciously recognise and differentiate between business as usual operations (BAU or 'running the business') and projects ('changing the business'). Each needs a different governance and management approach. Failure to understand this differentiation results in 'wastage' of resources and staff confusion. Organisations need to ensure that people who do both BAU and project activities have clearly defined performance criteria to ensure that motivations are aligned to the right outcomes from each. Organisations need to commit to project working and to be able to overlay project roles onto 'BAU job titles' and translate between the two. In the project world someone's 'BAU job title' is interesting but not as useful as their 3PM role title.

With maturity, most organisations quickly recognise the need for a formal framework for 3PM across the business, and also move to ensure that there is a 'line of sight' between every project and specific corporate objectives, in some cases via programmes. The same needs to be true for the line-of-sight accountability via governance roles from project team members, via a project/programme manager, sponsor and thence to the main board.

The crucial role of the board

A board sits at the apex of governance in any organisation and is responsible for risk oversight and maintaining sound systems of internal control. As such, the board is accountable for the overall governance of project management and must be convinced of the need for, and support of, a robust framework for 3PM. The board needs to define the portfolio direction for the business (set the strategic roadmap) and ensure that good organisational capability is in place.

In large organisations many of the day-to-day accountabilities of the board for 3PM governance can be delegated to a sub-committee of the board (such as an investment or change board or committee). However, the crucial link back to the main board needs to exist and the board members need to recognise their role and accountability at the apex of governance.

The board is responsible for 'picking' the right projects, ensuring that they go through robust business case assessments and that clear priorities are set and articulated. Once the corporate portfolio is established the board should regularly challenge the portfolio and individual projects, assure progress, create the 'environmental' support (and culture) and put in place the organisational capability. This is how the board controls the strategic roadmap and entry/exit of projects to ensure maximum value from the corporate portfolio.

Ten golden rules

From the research and my own experience I have captured ten golden rules for good governance (Table 7.1). I recommend that every organisation use these as the basis for assessing their project management governance maturity. The list is not exhaustive but represents the top ten areas that organisations should act upon to improve. Each is explained below.

Rule 1: Alignment and relationships

The PwC Survey (PwC, 2012) found that 'there is an emerging trend towards strategic portfolio management functions' and that effective 'Portfolio Management

TABLE 7.1 Ten golden rules for good governance

1	Alignment and relationships
2	Vision and strategic roadmap
3	Golden thread of delegation
4	Framework, process and decision gates
5	Clearly allocated roles
6	Requirements: keeping the end destination in sight
7	Transparent reporting
8	Capacity and competence
9	Assurance
10	Leadership, collaboration and supportive culture.

is becoming a competitive differentiator'. Companies that are poorly aligned with strategy reported weaker financial results than their peers. Subsequent surveys reveal that 'only 62% of programmes have an established or mature link between programme objectives and organisational strategy and only 50% of the respondents felt that the boundaries of their organisations portfolio were clearly defined and decision making well supported' (PwC, 2014).

The board must recognise and ensure a strong link between each project in the portfolio and its intended impact on strategic objectives. In turn, each board member and each project or programme sponsor should be able to articulate clearly how each project or programme is aligned with strategic objectives and will affect strategic key performance indicators. The board should define and own the entry, exit and prioritisation criteria for the portfolio. That requires regular challenges and reviews (at least quarterly), with a clear methodology to ensure maximum alignment. The board should be aware of the constraints on the major projects and how they are being addressed.

Each board member and sponsor should have identified, and be engaging with, key stakeholders, ensuring they can see how the changes/projects impact on organisational objectives in order to gain their support.

At the project level the team benefits from a strong alignment with strategic objectives as they can more easily resist challenge from external sources and proceed with the minimum interference and readjustment.

Rule 2: Vision and strategic roadmap

A key board role is to set the strategic direction of the business and the roadmap to achieve the goals. The board should have hands-on engagement with the corporate portfolio of projects; or at least have a solid overview, with hands-on engagement with the *vital few* highly strategic or high-risk programmes, and other oversight delegated to a board sub-committee.

At all three levels of portfolio, programme and project (3P) there should be a clear vision or 'end state' that defines clearly the destination for each (e.g. market positioning, target operating model, etc.). The overall method for the journey towards the vision must be clearly articulated and understood by the team and stakeholders. At portfolio level, the board owns and articulates the vision. The relevant sponsor has this role at the programme and project level.

Another key decision at the outset of a project is choosing the most appropriate delivery method. For example, choosing a traditional 'waterfall'-type approach to deliver into a rapidly changing environment, where the objective and method of getting to the result is uncertain, is likely to lead to project failure because the rate of change might outpace the rate of progress on the project. In this circumstance the board ought to consider the merits of using an incremental delivery or a programme-oriented approach, like MSP, DSDM, or Agile. References for DSDM and MSP are given at the end of this chapter. Specific guidelines for the governance of Agile projects are available from the APM. The important issue is matching the method to the circumstances and challenges – and ensuring that the governance regime matches the delivery method and remains flexible.

Rule 3: Golden thread of delegation

A key part of governance is to delegate an appropriate level of executive power to the key managers. Delegate too little, and the manager's freedom will be excessively constrained. Delegating too much risks that managers and the board will lose touch with each other.

It is vital that each key governance role aligns with another for accountability. Organisations should have a systematic and documented corporate governance policy defining where (body or role in the organisation) each type of change (3PM) decisions can be most effectively made, by whom and to what authority level (often defined by financial limits). Often organisations do have financial approval limits set by job description or seniority in the organisation – but for the 3PM governance world this needs to be also by project role – for example, sponsor, project manager, stage review panel.

There should be a hierarchy of accountability in the way each level in the organisational hierarchy is granted defined responsibilities and powers. It is important that each level and person understands the expectations regarding their responsibilities in order that accountability leads to the most appropriate behaviours. That of course applies to any business organisation.

A basic principle of good governance is that no one individual should have unfettered power over decision making. Checks or audits should exist that oversee the actions of individuals. Big decisions should be made on a collective basis. The corollary to this is that the board maintains effective oversight of delegated decisions – receiving information, challenging, assuring and supporting to evaluate the effectiveness of performance and behaviour.

Rule 4: Framework, process and decision gates

As stated previously, organisations need a framework that recognises and distinguishes projects from BAU. Organisations that aspire to good governance go much further than this. They develop a comprehensive framework of life cycles, defined role descriptions, 3PM governance roles, rules and detailed processes to ensure consistency of application and language across an organisation.

A crucial element of this framework is to have review and decision gates that all projects progress through (also known in some organisations as stage gates) to ensure that all projects are reviewed objectively by the business at key points in their life cycles. Good governance will specify when these critical decisions need to be made and name those involved in making them. Decision gates operate at three levels:

1   at portfolio level, to enable controlled entry and exit of projects to realise maximum value and monitoring and forecasting of strategic outcomes – where *failing early* is the new success;
2   at programme level, to enable a clear business blueprint or target operating model, strategy, appropriate funding and benefits delivery at specific gates;
3   at project level, to enable appropriate definition, development of information, business case and delivery of 'product' at each gate. A particular focus for projects is to ensure that the appropriate level of focus is given to the 'front end'. Rushing into implementation without ensuring solid definition up front is always a false economy on projects. If the project is doomed to failure, then 'failing early' and cancelling the project is best in the long-term interests of the organisation. And if adopting an Agile approach then 'time boxing' is crucial – for example, delay to a planned 'Gate Review' is unacceptable.

There should be consistent processes at all three levels to ensure consistency and address, for example, funding, reporting, quality, stakeholder, risk, value, benefits, cost, time and issues management.

The gate approval process should be carried out by competent senior managers to ensure that continuation of projects is in the best interests of the business. A Benchmarking Study of governance by the APM's Governance Specific Interest Group (SIG) found that 70 per cent of organisations had five or more gate reviews during a typical project.

Any framework should include targets for data collection, making key governance decisions and enacting them. Quick key decision making is particularly important in Agile projects (within 24 hours, for example).

Rule 5: Clearly allocated roles

Organisations need line-of-sight accountability from project team members, via a project manager, sponsor and thence to the main board. 3PM roles and responsibilities should be made clear and accountabilities allocated – aside from BAU job titles. Having clarity and avoiding overlap or gaps between role responsibilities is a crucial requirement for good governance and getting true accountability. I have seen many examples where, when things go wrong, key players are heard to say 'I didn't realise that was my responsibility'. In other cases an individual – often the project manager – is blamed for failure when it was, for example, the sponsor's responsibility.

Even if someone has a big job title in an organisation, the question should still be asked: 'what is their 3PM role and responsibility in the specific situation?' Only then can we be clear on who is accountable for making the key decisions.

So, both at project and programme levels we need to understand who the named individuals in the following roles are:

- sponsor or project executive (who may be supported by a sponsor team, steering committee or a project board). This is not to be confused with a stakeholder group;
- project manager;
- senior user;
- senior supplier.

The sponsor role is pivotal, as I would argue that six out of the eight causes of project failure outlined in the Introduction fall at the feet of the sponsor, not the project manager. Yet, despite this importance, the PMI *Pulse of the Profession* survey (PMI, 2014) showed that more than a third of projects do not have a clearly identified sponsor.

Sponsor continuity is also crucial. A change of sponsor mid-way through the project life cycle is often cited as a key reason for failure. An APM benchmarking study (APM, 2011) found that fewer than 25 per cent of projects have the same sponsor throughout. The NAO (2013) highlighted that the 'challenged' Universal Credit programme had no fewer than five different sponsors in 18 months. Change of sponsor should also be treated as a reason to 'relaunch' the project – going through the requirements, strategy and key success factors to ensure that the new sponsor is supportive.

We also need clear role definitions at the portfolio level, where the politics become ever more complicated. These roles need a clear linkage to individual programme and project governance – no matter where in the organisation they sit or are driven from. So we need to name the body and its membership that is responsible for selecting and prioritising the corporate portfolio of projects (for which the main board is accountable).

In this regard, the benchmarking study by the APM Governance SIG (APM, 2011) found that one of the key determinants of good governance was seen as having a project management representative on the board (a 'chief projects officer' or equivalent, for example). Over half of the organisations represented in the study had such a role.

Rule 6: Requirements: keeping the end destination in sight

Project management by definition is about achieving a result or change. So requirements definition and planning is crucial. But how many times do teams lose sight of the end objective or business case?

We carry out the task of planning by representing activities from today and then into the future – in the Western world, from 'left to right'. But we need to keep checking that the forecast result is still appropriate and that the 'left to right' activities, once completed, will result in the desired outcome. Hence we also need 'right to left' planning. This is essential in programmes, as the end result cannot be defined precisely at the outset and the programme will keep changing in shape as the team learns and the environment of the programme develops; then the need for 'right to left' planning and re-forecasting the outcome is even more important.

Traditionally, project practitioners like to 'lock things down' and are trained to define things in a progressive level of detail through a life cycle from concept through to testing and completion. 'Locking onto delivery' too early can mean that a subtle change to the environment into which you are delivering can result in the end product being perceived as a failure – failure to meet what is necessary. Good governance needs to overcome this propensity – and keep a focus on the end outcome and needs, especially if the environment is dynamic. In short, the higher-level governance bodies need to 'stay conscious', and to compensate for the lower levels sometimes becoming 'comatose'.

Throughout the endeavour key questions must be asked, and in a formal gate review setting as described above, about whether the desired outcome can still be met, the benefits are still on track, the method for delivery is still valid etc. This is a crucial role of governance – to *imagine failure* – involving people outside the endeavour but linked into the business (the review panel) – with the knowledge that the people associated with the core endeavour may not be able to see what an outsider can see. Ultimately the key driver for projects and programmes is the beneficial outcome.

At the portfolio level the board governance activity would be to constantly re-forecast and check to see if the desired business performance (the strategic objectives) can still be delivered within the dynamic business environment with the selected portfolio of projects. If not, the portfolio must be modified.

Rule 7: Transparent reporting

There must be transparency of change decisions or actions, and communication of their outcome using one version of the truth. Good governance should ensure that reporting is open and honest and there are clearly defined criteria for reporting 3P status and for the escalation of risks and issues to the levels required by the organisation.

The board has a key responsibility to set the appropriate reporting 'tone'. This should include ensuring that information published is suitable for easy absorption by the reader or audience. It should match the main measure of progress to the priority objectives – for example, time, cost, quality and benefits. In addition, the board should be explicit about 'whistle blowing' and reporting of bad news.

Reporting needs to be hierarchical. Each report should be specifically addressed to the audience it is intended to serve. Reports should be available, in the most appropriate format, to all the key stakeholders in order to ensure transparency.

Rule 8: Capacity and competence

A core area of governance is ensuring that appropriate numbers (capacity) and skilled and experienced resources (competence) are in place for delivering projects. People deliver projects! There must be enough of them – with competence in their roles and with the right tools.

We would not expect to win a football/soccer championship without competent players in the right positions on the pitch. Why, then, do we assume that we will have project success by fielding non-competent people on the 'project field'? In this respect the competence of all players, including sponsors, senior managers and board members, is vital. We can assume that these senior members of an organisation must be competent in their own domain to have risen to senior roles. But they all need to be competent in their new 'project roles'. This involves not just knowing the rules and language of the project game but having and practising the skill to achieve project success.

Good governance is not just about appointing a competent project manager. That player is just one of the players on the 'project pitch'. Good governance is also about ensuring that the other key players are competent in their roles and that they perform as a coherent and collaborative team.

A poll conducted by APM (2011) revealed that the key principle of directing change that gave organisations the most difficulty was the competence, authority and resources of decision makers. Both private and public sectors have invested heavily in increasing the competence of project managers in recent years, but less so in other roles. The most important of these other roles is the sponsor and the board/members at portfolio level. A series of studies have shown that, on average, 50 per cent of sponsors do not know what is expected of them or do not feel competent to carry out the role. An APM benchmarking study found that only 8 per cent of the organisations used a competency assessment model for selecting sponsors. Furthermore, only 40 per cent of the respondents had project benefits measures in their sponsors' personal performance measures.

We have already identified sponsor competence improvement as a key requirement for good governance (and project success) and an area for general improvement. Some organisations recognise this issue and are helping to build sponsor competence by having 'sponsor agents' (programme or business professionals to provide vital support to busy strategic sponsors) or sponsor coaches to help fill competency shortfalls.

The 2014 *Pulse of the Profession* survey (PMI, 2014) has demonstrated a direct correlation between effective talent management and better project performance. Organisations with the foresight to recognise that organisational capability improvement is a strategic objective appoint a 'chief projects officer' (or similar). They develop a community of project professionals and establish a 'centre of excellence' – opening project management academies to develop talent. They encourage and expect staff to join reputable professional institutes and gain formal qualifications as part of professionalising project management.

Rule 9: Assurance

Corroboration of project status through rigorous independent review is the penultimate golden rule. Again, the board (or its delegated sub-committee or sponsor) needs to decide when independent scrutiny of projects, programmes or project management systems is required and to implement such assurance accordingly. Independent scrutiny is a vital tool for the board to get a second opinion on the health of projects and project management in general. An independent view on a specific project does not necessarily mean using a body external to the organisation – a peer review might satisfy that need and increase cross-business learning or sharing.

Assurance is the final 'safety gate' for ensuring that a board or project/programme team has not become 'comatose' and lost sight of the desired outcome. A key assurance role is to ensure that the board is fully conscious of what is happening and making decisions accordingly.

But beware! Boards need also to ensure that they don't 'just' rely (or over-rely) on assurance reviews; these are often only a 'snapshot' in time. The board must remain conscious and ensure that other normal governance structures and reporting channels are also in place.

Rule 10: Leadership, collaboration and supportive culture

I have left this rule to last because it is the most important and has the greatest impact on effective governance. Put simply, good governance is all about how people behave. These behaviours need to be set from the top.

The board and sponsors have a crucial leadership role, not only in defining and motivating people to meet the overall goal and objectives, but also in setting the right culture to enable delivery.

The right culture has to be driven from the top, as the board members sit at the apex of governance. Only the senior people can set, reward and enforce a culture of transparency, openness, collaboration, performance focus, empowerment, single-point accountability, role adherence, ethical working and so on. The board members need to individually and collectively demonstrate good behaviours of governance. The board has to ensure that the policies, ethics, culture and 'tone' are set appropriately and that adherence to good governance principles is not compromised. Board members need to foster a culture of improvement and of frank internal disclosure of information. Board members, either directly or indirectly, influence this by what they say and what they do.

Improving and delivering good governance comes mainly through a change of culture, behaviours and relationships. Organisations do need a coherent structure and processes for project management and control that transcend the business, but they primarily need a culture and behaviour of people that actually believe in and want to do things in the right way. An organisation could have the best structure in the world, and all the right review/authorisation bodies set up, but if the behaviour is wrong (with someone wanting to 'play a game' or circumvent lessons learned and good practice), good governance is destroyed.

End-users are running today's business and often feel that they are too busy to spend time thinking about a project that will not deliver for some months or even years. But we all know that early user involvement is crucial to avoiding late user changes when they don't like the deliverable. Again, this message to emphasise the need for early user involvement, and the benefit, needs to come from the top.

I have written much about the role of sponsors on individual projects and their leadership role as being critical to directing the project team, via the project manager. However, that role also includes protecting the delivery team from organisational interference. The sponsor needs to lead from the front and champion their project at every opportunity, not only within the organisation, but also with key external stakeholders.

The key players

The key players that have a core governance role are shown in a simple governance structure (Figure 7.2). This is not an exhaustive list, as each organisation needs a governance framework that is proportionate to its needs. For example, the structure will be far larger for complex and multi-owned projects. The important requirement is that the roles, authority and accountability lines are clear.

How much governance is enough?

Organisations are often grappling with the question 'How much governance is necessary?' The answer will vary from one organisation to another. These factors have to be considered, including size, marketplace, stakeholders, maturity, appetite for risk, management style, history, personalities and competence. There is no one right way of delivering 'good' governance, but applying the basics and the suggested ten golden rules is crucial to making a good start.

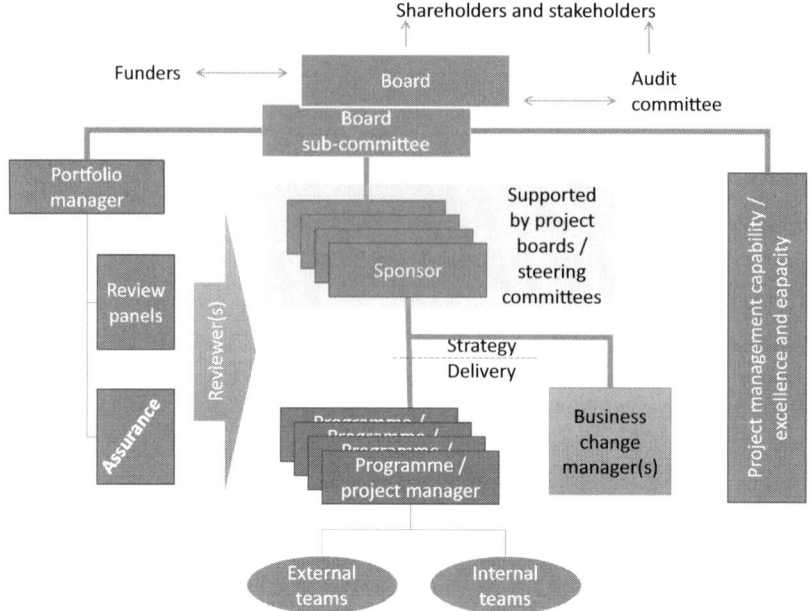

FIGURE 7.2 Key Governance Players and Accountability Lines

In smaller organisations the board would probably be intimately concerned with all its projects, but in bigger organisations with larger portfolios I would expect responsibility for governance to be delegated. However, the delegation must be in a hierarchy, where the board still has visibility of the most significant strategic projects and is assured that all others have an appropriate delegated level of governance with links back to the top.

The key requirement is that the governance framework should be proportionate and realistic. It should be structured and applied in a flexible and pragmatic manner. It is not an end in itself but a means of adding value to an organisation, providing continuity, increasing transparency and controlling risk.

Success

Summary

Success in project delivery has not improved markedly over the last few decades. The reasons for failed projects are the same now as then. Most of the causes are the responsibility of the governance of project management – and specifically the sponsors of projects and programmes and main board members. Good governance of project management is not a dream. By following the principles and golden rules outlined in this chapter, organisations can move toward better governance, and thence to more successful project outcomes.

Structure, process and tools are essential enablers to improve governance. However, the crucial enabler is the behaviour and leadership of the board or top team and project sponsors. Organisations need to make good governance a strategic objective. Directors and executives of organisations must stay conscious, avoid becoming 'comatose' and become more professional in their roles associated with projects and change. Above all, *the* key success factor in projects is having an engaged and effective sponsor.

Two simple suggestions

There is no magic bullet for project success. However, to counter governance (project) failures, I suggest two simple interventions to make a difference.

First, I have focused this chapter on the role of the board or executive team. However, project managers also need to take some responsibility for governance and project failure. They often spot issues of poor governance but do nothing about it, as they feel impotent. My message to project managers is to be more challenging and demanding of their organisation. Use the rules and principles of good governance, spread the word, hold them up to those responsible for governance and ask them to challenge themselves as to how they are doing. Attaining good governance is a journey to which all must contribute.

Second, at the starting point of each project the senior team must be a little more circumspect and *imagine failure*. Instead of thinking that everything is going to go right, imagine the worst-case scenario: challenge the sponsor, reflect on the normal reasons for failure, revisit lessons learned from previous projects and ask what special steps are being taken in order to address the normal reasons for failure up front.

During the rest of the project ensure that they and their colleagues remain conscious – things will change, but keep asking the same questions. This simple good governance approach can be taken by any board or senior leadership team. Also, in this small this way they can demonstrate their overall responsibility and proactivity.

Ultimately the board is accountable for good governance and has to ensure the right process, competencies, culture and behaviours are in place.

References

APM. (2011). *Directing change*. Princes Risborough: Association for Project Management.

APM. (2012). *APM body of knowledge* (6th ed.). Princes Risborough: Association for Project Management.

APM. (2015). *Factors in project success*. Princes Risborough: Association for Project Management.

DSDM. (2014). *Agile project framework*. London: DSDM.

FRC. (2012). *The UK corporate governance code*. London: Financial Reporting Council.

IOD. (2010). *Corporate governance guidance and principles for unlisted companies in the UK*. London: Institute of Directors.

ISO 21505. (2017). *Project, programme and portfolio management – Guidance on governance.* Geneva, Switzerland: International Standards Organization.

ISO/IEC 38500. (2015). *Information technology – Governance of IT for the organization.* Geneva, Switzerland: International Standard Organization.

NAO. (2012). *Lessons from cancelling the intercity West Coast franchise competition.* London: National Audit Office.

NAO. (2013). *Universal credit: Early progress.* London: National Audit Office.

OECD. (2004). *Principles of corporate governance.* Paris: OECD.

OGC. (2007). *Managing successful programmes.* London: The Stationery Office.

OGC. (2009). *Prince 2.* London: The Stationery Office.

PMI. (2014). *Pulse of the profession: The high cost of low performance.* Newton Square, PA: Project Management Institute.

PMI. (2015). *Guide to the project management body of knowledge (PMBoK)* (5th ed.). Newton Square, PA: Project Management Institute.

PwC. (2012). *3rd global portfolio and programme management survey.* London: PwC.

PwC. (2014). *4th global portfolio and programme management survey.* London: PwC.

8
Change

WHO KILLED CHANGE? RECONSIDERING THE RELATIONSHIP BETWEEN PROJECTS AND CHANGE

Darren Dalcher

Society is full of potential change agents agitating for improvement, enhancement and further development. Aspirant initiatives range from improving public services, reforming government and available services and engaging younger voters in politics, to the transformation of organisations, the successful implementation of mergers and acquisitions and the development of digital presence, experiences and perspectives to corporate life, social communities and consumer behaviours. Yet, while change is ubiquitous to thriving societal and organisational life, change initiatives continue to flounder at an alarming rate. The poor success rate of change initiatives has intrigued change management and organisational psychology research-ers and practitioners for over half a century. This chapter focuses on some of the leading insights into change management and its successful adoption.

Leading change

In 1995, Harvard Business School professor John Kotter published the results of a ten-year study of more than 100 companies that had attempted major organisational transformations and turnaround projects (Kotter, 1995). His research highlighted the eight most significant errors made by organisations seeking to implement change programmes that can doom any change effort (and are slightly enhanced and expanded below):

Error 1: Not establishing a great enough sense of urgency: Often augmented by underestimating the difficulty of driving people from their comfort zone, or becoming paralysed by risks.

Error 2: Not creating a powerful enough guiding coalition: Potentially relegating change leadership to a functional manager, instead of seeking a senior line manager or sponsor with the ability to connect across silos and functional units.

Error 3: Lacking a vision: Presenting a vision that is too complicated or vague to be communicated briefly and effectively.

Error 4: **Under-communicating the vision**: May include missing opportunities to sell and present the change, settling on a single communication channel (e.g. a single meeting or one leaflet), or not getting executives to behave in ways that support the proposals.

Error 5: Not removing obstacles to the new vision: Obstacles may include organisational structures, culture, processes, systems or individuals, and may thus require changes to risk-taking approaches, and the acceptance of radical or revamped approaches and ways of thinking.

Error 6: Not systematically planning for, and creating, short-term wins: Transformation takes time, so potential pitfalls to success may hinge on not including visible short-terms goals that can demonstrate achievement, failing to provide compelling evidence of success and failing to identify and score success early enough in the process.

Error 7: Declaring victory too soon: Not recognising that early performance improvements are only early wins, and thereby leading to failure to consolidate improvements and deliver more of the agreed-upon change.

Error 8: Not anchoring changes in the corporation's culture: Potential failure to create new social norms and shared values consistent with the required change, or failure to promote and create a succession plan that is consistent with the new transformation.

Kotter maintained that many managers failed to recognise that transformation is a process rather than an event:

> The most general lesson to be learned from the most successful cases is that the change process goes through a series of phases that, in total, usually require a considerable length of time. Skipping steps creates only the illusion of speed and never produces satisfying results. A second very general lesson is that critical mistakes in any of the phases can have a devastating impact, slowing momentum and negating hard-won gains.
>
> (Kotter, 1995, p. 59)

Realising that implementing change takes a long time can therefore improve the chances of success. Successful delivery of change requires advancing through stages (roughly corresponding to the errors discussed above) that build on one another. According to Kotter, pressures to accelerate and fast-track the process will encourage managers and leaders to skip steps, and these shortcuts are ultimately likely to lead to failure . . .

So, who killed change?

Change is often devised in order to improve the status quo, but the mere intention to effect such change invokes opposing emotions and feelings and fosters active and intentional resistance. Italian diplomat, politician and philosopher Niccoló Machiavelli memorably wrote: 'There is nothing more difficult to take in hand, more perilous to conduct, or more uncertain in its success than to take the lead in the introduction of a new order of things.'

Change is intrinsically difficult. Kotter and Cohen (2002) asserted that in order to make a transformation endeavour successful, one must change more than just the structure and operations of an organisation; indeed, the key challenge is to change people's behaviour. Garvin and Roberto (2005) likewise identified the key obstacle as the reluctance of most people to alter their habits:

> What worked in the past is good enough; in the absence of a dire threat, employees will keep doing what they have always done. And when an organization has had a succession of leaders, resistance to change is even stronger. A legacy of disappointment and distrust creates an environment in which employees automatically condemn the next turnaround champion to failure.
>
> (Ibid., p. 26)

Ken Blanchard and his colleagues offered an novel perspective on the issues impacting on change initiatives (Blanchard et al., 2009). Their published book features yet another failed change initiative with a hero attempting to solve the mystery of *Who Killed Change?*

The unfolding mystery, described in the style of a business whodunit, offers insights into change. The investigating agent examines the scene and is able to identify 13 potential suspects most likely to have been involved in the snuffing-out of change. The full list of suspects features a number of familiar faces encompassing culture, commitment, sponsorship, change leadership team, communication, urgency, vision, plan, budget, trainer, incentive, performance management and accountability. The unfolding case depicts shortfalls in all 13 areas, drawing suspicion to each and all of the suspect characters. For example, Clair Communication is suffering from laryngitis. Change, it appears, cannot survive when communication is faulty or non-existent. Perry Plan is always late, thereby continually disappointing all interested parties. Victoria Vision is myopic: if vision cannot see properly it is unable to support its role. Meanwhile, Earnest Urgency is always late and fails to inculcate the dire need for change.

The story also encompasses additional witnesses, the stakeholders, and their view of the demise of change. The stakeholders assert that there are a number of barriers that are mostly ignored by senior and middle management, which are observable only by front-line employees and engaged supervisors. The stakeholders see a different side of change that is not visible to the senior management team.

Many factors can contribute to the failure of change initiatives. Indeed, all the aforementioned characters play a part in the death of change, by combining their flaws and impacts to suffocate the initiative. The short answer to who killed change is everybody, through acting together and interacting.

However, the autopsy report compiled by the investigating agent identifies three perilous, yet typical, assumptions.

- People leading the change think that announcing it is the same as integrating it.
- People's concerns with change are not surfaced or addressed.
- Those being asked to implement change are not involved in the planning.

The assumptions appear to hold true for many organisations and change endeavours, offering a further understanding of the shortfalls of change efforts.

Where is the project manager?

Reassuringly, the project manager was not one of the characters directly responsible for the failure (arguably because they were not around when the change was conceived – or when the business case was being developed).

However, change management is increasingly creeping into the discussion surrounding the success of projects. Project managers join the dance of change further downstream when many aspects are already defined, agreed and in play. They are increasingly called upon to utilise change management approaches to address the softer aspects of change, leadership and stakeholder engagement, and directly engage with all the normal suspects.

Yet, there is little guidance within the profession regarding the role of change in projects. This chapter by Nicola Busby begins to address this gap. The work is developed from her book, *The Shape of Change* (2017), published by Routledge. Busby draws attention to the scope of business change in projects. Her worked example shows the importance of understanding the impact of change, not just from a practical perspective. Indeed, by employing strategic tools, she is able to show a need to consider wider aspects of leadership, culture and behaviours that contribute to the demise of change. Above all, the example confirms that if we change the way we look at things, the things we look at (and therefore the potential ways of addressing them) change.

Busby's work supports the change journey of organisations and initiatives from a pragmatic and workable perspective that enables change agents to shape their efforts and tailor their approaches to delivering change. Her focus on stakeholders and their role is essential to making sense of engagement and resistance, laying the foundations for addressing support, communication and learning needs within organisations that are seeking to keep change alive and well.

The value of the approach is in highlighting essential aspects of a project that cannot be accessed through typical project management routines or expectations, thereby augmenting existing approaches and encouraging a longer-term perspective on change.

Russian author count Lev Nikolayevich Tolstoy, better known as Leo Tolstoy, lamented that 'everyone thinks about changing the world, but no one thinks of changing himself'. Professionals often need to change themselves and their approaches in order to improve, develop and fundamentally alter their performance. Busby's book encourages project managers to consider the impact and scope of change and develop new and informed approaches that are able to leverage the new understanding in order to enhance change efforts and their likelihood of succeeding.

Reprising change

Project managers are increasingly aware that the success of their projects and resulting products extends beyond technical implementation and handover. Indeed, the success of many change efforts relies on the outputs being utilised and used regularly in order to deliver the stream of benefits and thus realise the promised value. Such changes in behaviour and the acceptance of new patterns of engaging with systems and technologies can be enacted only through engagement with stakeholders and users. They also imply understanding organisational, cultural and social expectations and norms and working to deliver meaningful and sustainable change.

Change is messy and frustrating, often requiring muddling through and making sense of the participants and their preferences, unpicking the individual needs and priorities and the different aspects and contextual elements of a situation. When change efforts fail, it can prove extremely difficult to untangle the diverse influences and priorities of the various actors and participants and determine conclusively who killed change.

Yet, identifying the culprit is less important than avoiding the unfortunate death of change endeavours. It is typically reckoned that, at the very least, two-thirds of change initiatives flounder. Developing a range of new perspectives and extending our repertoire to encompass change management tools and frameworks may not eliminate the death of all change initiative, but can make a new start towards reducing the list of 'usual suspects' that threaten the health of new change efforts. It can also encourage society, the economy and our corporations to aim higher and deliver more sustainable, more prosperous and more meaningful and relevant change endeavours.

References

Blanchard, K., Britt, J., Hoekstra, J. & Zigarmi, P. (2009). *Who killed change?* New York: HarperCollins.

Busby, N. (2017). *The shape of change: A guide to planning, implementing and embedding organisational change.* Abingdon: Routledge.

Garvin, D. A. & Roberto, M. A. (2005). Change through persuasion. *Harvard Business Review, 83,* 26–33.

Kotter, J. P. (1995). Leading change: Why transformation efforts fail. *Harvard Business Review,* 73(2), 59–67.

Kotter, J. P. & Cohen, D. S. (2002). *The heart of change: Real-life stories of how people change their organizations.* Cambridge, MA: Harvard Business Press.

THE VALUE OF BUSINESS CHANGE MANAGEMENT IN PROJECTS

Nicola Busby

It is an exciting time to be working in business change. Over the past few years interest in the profession has increased exponentially. Organisations that still struggle to realise the expected benefits of their changes, despite increasingly sophisticated project frameworks, are exploring its potential as the missing link to success. Job vacancies for business change managers are on the increase. The role itself is professionalising with representation from at least two global bodies, each of which has developed a change management body of knowledge. There are a number of accredited training and development paths for those who wish to enter and progress in the field. Alongside this are a wealth of consultancies that can support organisations going through change with bespoke approaches, methodologies, philosophies and frameworks. There is a lot of investment in business change right now.

My years of work, training and research in business change management leave me convinced that the only way to introduce successful change into organisations is through a concentrated focus on the people involved. Therefore, I am thrilled about the increased interest in business change management. However, the rapid development of the profession is beginning to resemble a Chinese dragon – a small head at the front with a very long tail trailing along behind. The trailblazers are coming up with more and more sophisticated approaches, terminologies and frameworks for business change, whilst a large percentage are struggling to keep up.

This means that many of those who should be benefiting from the increased investment in business change remain largely in ignorance about what business change management can achieve, or hold outdated assumptions about what it is and what it does. This seems to be true of both those working in organisations which are experiencing change and those working in the field of change itself – in the world of projects and programmes. Even business change managers don't always seem to be fully aware of how powerful their role can be, and how they are often the key to successful organisational change.

One common situation where people struggle is how to utilise business change management within projects. Most project managers expect to undertake some stakeholder engagement and communications as part of their role. In fact, project management best practice, training qualifications and bodies of knowledge are increasingly being revised to include people aspects of change. So, how and why can a business change manager add value to a project?

The scope of business change management in a project

There are generally three things to focus on in a project, as shown in Figure 8.1.

The object of the change is the thing that is changing. This could be anything from a software upgrade to a new target operating model, or a focus on a new customer segment.

The associated activities are the things that people will need to do differently to work with the object of the change successfully.

The people involved in the change. For change to be successful, every individual required to plan, make decisions and implement the change needs to be supportive and contribute effectively. Every user affected by the change needs to make the decision to participate and make the effort to do things differently. These are the areas which are the domain of the business change manager.

Organisational change is tough. It can be contentious, emotive, unpopular and sheer hard work. By its very nature, change often disturbs deep-rooted values and cultures. It rarely benefits everyone it touches and often raises the tensions and insecurities which bubble just below the surface of many organisations. It is in these situations that business change managers really add value. They can build desire for change, overcome resistance, increase involvement and ownership and

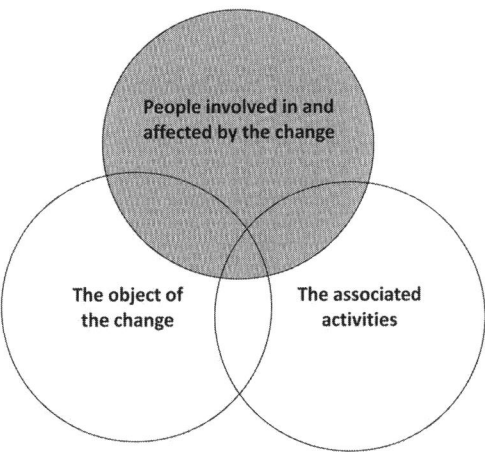

FIGURE 8.1 The scope of business change

make people feel more positive about the change. Positivity significantly increases the chances of the organisation accepting the change, embedding it and realising its benefits.

Obviously, some projects are not as contentious or challenging as others. Therefore, the degree to which business change intervention is needed varies widely. However, it is surprising how often a supposedly straightforward change can actually impact upon people in very deep ways. This is illustrated in the case study below.

Case study: Changing financial reporting systems at Fortisdown Energy[1]

Fortisdown Energy is a large energy company situated in the north-east of England. Established in the 1960s, it develops alternative energy products and generates energy which is used to supply homes and businesses in the local area. It has a worldwide reputation as innovative and imaginative, producing world-leading research and development in the alternative energy sector.

Historically, Fortisdown has received large amounts of development funding from the UK government, in addition to significant research grants from other sources. It also generates a modest income from sales of its energy to the National Grid.

Over the decade since 2008 the UK government has reduced its funding and has indicated that further reductions are likely. Research grants have also decreased, due in part to increased competition from newer alternative energy companies. Fortisdown is therefore facing severe budget shortfalls over the next few years.

In order to make up this shortfall in income, the CEO decided that the entire company needs to become more efficient, and spending needs to become more transparent and brought under control.

The change Initiative

To help with this efficiency drive, the executive team agreed to implement a new company-wide financial reporting system. The aims of this were to:

- increase transparency of financial interactions across Fortisdown in order to boost efficiency and reduce spend;
- create management reports to help with financial forecasting and yearly budget setting.

An off-the-shelf financial system was purchased and implementation commenced. The engagement plan developed by the project team focused on informing people about the change, training all users in how to use the new system and ensuring that everyone knew how to prepare to move from the old system to the new one.

As the project progressed, the project team began to meet a lot of resistance from users across the company, especially in the research and development teams. People did not engage in preparation activities and attendance at training sessions was low. Interaction with the project team was minimal and staff seemed reluctant to enter financial data into the new system. The project team began to doubt that the new system would be adopted fully across the company. This meant that, even if the system was implemented successfully onto the technology infrastructure, lack of use would lead to project failure – the benefits of the new system would not be realised.

Therefore, they brought in a business change manager to try to manage the resistance to the project. One of the first things she did was to analyse the culture of the organisation and research the circumstances leading up to the change project. She then undertook a thorough impact assessment for the project using the 7S model to analyse the impact of the change initiative on the company. The results were surprising to the project team.

What is the 7S model?

The McKinsey 7S model (Waterman and Peters, 1982) is an effective tool to use for an impact assessment. It allows the impact of the change to be examined from seven different aspects of an organisation, as follows.

1   **Strategy:** the plan of how to run the organisation successfully.
2   **Structure:** organisation charts and who reports to whom.
3   **Systems:** formal processes and systems such as IT, rewards and measurement.
4   **Style:** leadership styles found within the organisation.
5   **Staff:** the general capabilities of the staff.
6   **Skills:** the actual skills and competencies of everyone working for the company.
7   **Shared values:** the culture and core values of the organisation.

The real strength of the 7S model is that it focuses on the impact of the change on behaviours, culture and values as well as the more tangible areas such as structures and systems. The more esoteric aspects of the organisation are often neglected during change, but it is vital to focus on them in order to minimise resistance and maximise the chances of successful benefits realisation.

To carry out an impact assessment using the 7S model, first analyse the differences which the change will bring to the seven aspects of the organisation by:

- listing what happens now – the current state;
- identifying what is expected to happen after the change – the future state; and,
- comparing the difference between the two – the gap.

TABLE 8.1 Fortisdown impact assessment

7S aspect	Current state	Future state	Gap	Size of impact
Strategy	Focus is on innovation and world-class research and development	Quality and type of research to be balanced with financial considerations	Need to understand financial impact of all work and prioritise accordingly	High
Systems	Financial reporting done on a range of systems across the organisation and to varying levels of detail. No detailed management reporting on finances available	New financial system for entire organisation. Detailed management reports will be available	New system to be implemented and old systems removed	Medium
Structure	Administrative roles input financial data in departments. Central finance team sets budgets and monitors finances	Administrative roles continue to input data in departments. Central finance team restructured in line with roles needed for new system	Restructured central finance team	Low
Style	Leadership focused on enabling high-quality research and development. Innovation encouraged and all resource constraints overcome. Research and development projects regularly run over time and budget	Leadership focused on balancing quality with cost. Financial implications of all decisions to be understood. Projects to have strong governance and controls to prevent overrun and overspending	Move from innovation and quality at any cost to working within clear boundaries with tight controls. Need to say 'no' to ideas and projects, or constrain them due to cost implications	High

Element	Current situation	Desired situation	Actions required	Significance
Staff	Capabilities in cutting-edge energy research and development	Capabilities in commercial, business-oriented thinking Increased financial and project management capabilities	Two new capabilities need to be introduced which will have equal importance to the capability in research and development	High
Skills	Strong skills in innovation, research and development Minimal skills in financial reporting and financial-focused decision making	Strong skills in innovation, research and development Strong skills in financial reporting and commercial decision making Skills needed in governing and controlling projects Technical skills in using new financial reporting system	Skills development needed in: financial reporting commercial decision making governance and control of projects new financial system usage	High
Shared values	Pride in undertaking cutting-edge, world-class research and development in alternative energy Success means overcoming all barriers to allow focus on research and development Resource constraints are a barrier and must be overcome	Pride in producing good-quality research and development whilst maintaining a financially secure business Success means being commercially aware and using resources wisely and efficiently	Move from belief in innovation and quality at any cost to valuing good quality within a culture of efficiency and value for money	High

Once this is completed, decide how significant the gap is for each of the seven aspects. A simple way to do this is to use the scale of high, medium, low or no change. An overall picture of the impact of the change on the organisation can then be seen.

Fortisdown impact assessment

Table 8.1 shows the impact assessment completed by the business change manager for the Fortisdown financial system change.

What the impact assessment revealed

The impact assessment revealed that Fortisdown would be hugely impacted by the change, in ways initially unforeseen by the project team. They had been focusing on the practical aspects of the initiative – implementing the new system and training everyone in how to use it. However, these were shown by the impact assessment to be the lowest areas of impact for the organisation. The focus actually needed to be on the more intangible areas of culture, behaviours, capabilities and values, which would all be highly impacted by the change.

This seemingly straightforward software implementation project, once analysed in depth, is actually a major cultural change. The resistance experienced by the project team was a signal that the impact on end-users was much greater than they had initially thought. In the end, the project had to invest heavily in business change management activities and increase its timescales significantly so as to support the changes in cultures and values needed for the project to become a success.

Conclusion

This case study illustrates how business change management can significantly increase the chances of a project being implemented successfully. Projects, by their very nature, often change the way things are done in an organisation, disturbing deep-rooted cultures, behaviours and values. In these situations, there is a need for much more focus on the people side of change than standard project management can offer.

Business change managers see the project through the eyes of the stakeholders and focus solely on mitigating negative impacts on people, and building support and buy-in for the change. This begins at the planning stage of the project and continues until the change has been implemented and is operating as business as usual. For projects which have a large impact on the people involved, it is only through this intense focus on the people side of the change that resistance can be minimised, the change can be embedded within the organisation and the benefits can be realised.

Note

1   Some names and details have been altered to protect anonymity.

References

Waterman, R. & Peters, T. (1982). *In search of excellence*. New York: Collins.

9
Commercial management

COMMERCIAL MANAGEMENT AND PROJECTS: A LONG OVERDUE MATCH?

Darren Dalcher

A search for the phrase 'commercial management' in the digital version of the 6th edition of PMI Guide released in 2017 fails to come up with a single result. The 6th edition of *Body of Knowledge* from the UK's Association for Project Management similarly offers no matches. The leading canons of project management knowledge would thus seem to imply that commercial management has nothing whatsoever to do with projects. The apparent disconnect is a little troubling, since commercial management has a lot to offer project management practitioners and researchers.

The ignorance of commercial management is even more puzzling, given that over the years a number of decent books have endeavoured to bridge that gap, offering treatises that address the links, connections and common issues. Perhaps the first book to offer such insight and focus on the area is *The Commercial Project Manager* edited by Professor Rodney Turner in 1995. The Foreword to the book, written by Dr Martin Barnes, former president of the UK's Association for Project Management, notes that 'many projects are not managed with proper consideration of commercial aspects. Only in the last few years have many people realized, for example, that only the most trivial projects are completed without needing well designed contracts between the contributing people and organizations.'

Dr Barnes uses the analogy of risk management, which had previously been considered as a 'bolt on extra' to project management technique, to highlight the need to similarly integrate commercial management into the very core of project management. More critically, he points out that rather than simply fill a gap, Turner's book first demonstrates an unrecognised gap before duly proceeding to fill it.

> Rodney Turner and his team have not taken up space with descriptions of the traditional techniques of project management. . . . But, for the first time, almost everything which sets the context within which these basic project management functions have to be performed is here. Reading *The Commercial*

> *Project Manager* starkly demonstrates how important the surrounding
> commercial considerations are to successful project management. Integration
> of the commercial aspects of the basic technology has often not been
> achieved. Full integration, based on a clear understanding makes a big
> difference to the success of the completed project. Strangely, this applies
> whether the objectives of the project are themselves intensely commercial
> or not.
>
> (Barnes, 1995, p. xiii)

Despite the clear potential impact on the profession, well over 20 years following
the publication of Professor Turner's book on the subject and the plea from Dr
Barnes, commercial management remains a relatively perplexing conundrum, still
completely unrecognised by the traditional project management sources of wisdom.

What is commercial management?

The Institute for Commercial Management (ICM), established in the 1970s and
currently based in Ringwood, Hampshire in the United Kingdom, purports to be
the leading international body for commercial and business development staff. Its
definition of commercial management positions it as: 'the identification and
development of business opportunities and the profitable management of projects
and contracts, from inception to completion' (ICM, 2017, p. 2).

While the roles within commercial management may be varied, individuals
take responsibility for sales, marketing, contracting, negotiations, contract law or
property management. According to the ICM, commercial managers 'ensure that
a project runs smoothly from inception to completion'. ICM further maintains
that a commercial manager is therefore 'someone whose primary role is in the
management or execution of such opportunities or projects' (ibid., p. 4). The key
knowledge areas highlighted in its publications feature commercial awareness,
contracts, contract performance, commercial relationships, negotiation, risk
management, post-delivery risk, project planning, team building and project
progression. The International Association for Contract and Commercial
Management also endeavours to support organisations and professionals to achieve
world-class standards in their contracting and relationship management process
and skills.

In positioning his book on the topic, David Lowe contends that the term
'commercial management' has been used for some time, not least in construction,
while the title of *commercial manager* can be found across a spectrum of industries,
especially those that are predominantly project based, including aerospace,
construction, IT, pharmaceutical and telecommunications (Lowe, 2008, p. vii).
Given that projects play a key part in executing organisational strategies, 'the
commercial management function is vital in linking operations at the project level
and multiple projects (portfolios/programmes) at the organisational level with the
organisational (corporate) core of the company. The function therefore can be

found at the interfaces between organisations as well as between divisions within an organisation' (ibid.).

Acknowledging the relative paucity of literature in the area, commercial management is thus defined as: 'the management of contractual and commercial issues relating to projects, from project inception to completion' (Lowe & Leiringer, 2008, p. 11).

Lowe and Leiringer (2005; 2008) reason that commercial management can be identified as a stand-alone discipline within project-based organisations, which bridges traditional project management with organisational theories. Whilst it typically encompasses contract management and dispute resolution, it may also address financial and value management and bid management within certain domains. It is noteworthy that whilst commercial management may not form an explicit part of the single project setup, it none the less holds a crucial role within project-based organisations and project-based industries in facilitating the commercial management of projects.

No project is an island

Turner (1995) positions his book, *The Commercial Project Manager*, by recognising that in reality no one organisation has all the available resources required to undertake a complete project in its entirety. Indeed, material, labour or professional services will often need to be sourced externally:

> Hence, project managers must develop their commercial skills to manage the relationship with external parties involved in a project, and the project's links with its context and environment.
>
> (Turner, 1995, p. xv)

Moreover, Turner (ibid.) acutely recognises that the majority of the literature in the project management area treats the project as an island, totally isolated from other actions, activities, events or structures. However, the project can no longer be considered an island. The introduction by Dr Barnes points out that it is both refreshing and exciting for commercial issues to take the centre stage.

> *The Commercial Project Manager* belongs to a mature phase of project management into which we have now moved. . . . [P]roject management is no longer an island; when placed within its surrounding commercial context, it becomes a valuable part of nearly everything we do.
>
> (Barnes, 1995, pp. xiii–xiv)

Dr Barnes's sentiment reflects a yearning for better-informed project management approaches. Welcoming the arrival of the new era 20-some years ago, may have been premature, as commercial management is yet to be integrated into the core of project management.

No longer on the periphery?

But perhaps commercial management is an overdue concept whose time and potential for recognition amongst project practitioners has finally arrived. The chapter by Robin Hornby aims to reinvigorate the passion for the area by emphasising its importance. Hornby embraces the leadership role required to initiate a further discussion about the potential impact of the discipline. The chapter is developed from his book *Commercial Project Management: A Guide for Selling and Delivering Professional Services*, published by Routledge.

Hornby (2017) firmly believes that the poor track record of project delivery can be improved by addressing the commercial concerns related to the context of projects. Selling and delivering a project to a satisfied client, and making a profit, are complex tasks that have been sadly neglected by the existing standards, methodologies and approaches, and consequently are poorly understood by practitioners. Hornby's approach combines practical case studies with pragmatic solutions and new ideas for addressing the commercial side of delivery and the continuous perspective of commercial relationships.

At the core of his approach, Hornby emphasises a sales and delivery life cycle, thereby providing a framework for business and commercial control of projects. He also recasts project management as a cyclic set of functions devised to lead the work of the projects against the backdrop of commercial emphasis. Crucially, he also provides new structures, approaches and insights for strengthening the commercial integration, viability and ability required to deliver projects successfully. The perspective repositions the architecture of the commercial project environment as capable of addressing the relationships between vendor life cycles, project life cycles used for the execution phase and core practices. It also provides the foundation for developing the concept and principles of total collaborative procurement as a methodology and approach for delivering services.

By placing commercial management at the core of delivery and relationships, it thus becomes possible to question the key assumptions and traditional models and to begin to construct a new reality of project (and business) delivery. By focusing on business aspects it may also be possible to emphasise new ways of developing, growing and sustaining success in projects.

One of the endorsements of Hornby's book comes from R. Max Wideman, past president of PMI and a leading authority and founding developer of the early version of the PMI's guide to the *Body of Knowledge*. Wideman notes that 'it is refreshing to find in this latest book, . . . a side of project management that is rarely tackled. In fact it is not about project management per se, but rather about how to make money, or certainly not to lose it.'

It would appear that recognition of the key role of commercial management and the need to rethink project work materialises on an intermittent basis, probably about once a decade. The discussion about creating connections with commercial management is long overdue and merits serious consideration. Returning the focus to this critical area and placing it squarely at the core of project discourse could prove to be an important step in repositioning projects and their management as the key to future growth, societal prosperity and organisational development. It may also finally signal the growing maturity of the discipline and the discourse it fosters. Ultimately, it may begin to remind us of why we do project work, and how we can become (even) better at it.

References

APM.

Barnes, M. (1995). Foreword. In J. R. Turner (Ed.), *The commercial project manager. Managing owners, sponsors, partners, supporters, stakeholders, contractors and consultants*. Maidenhead: McGraw Hill.

Hornby, R. (2017). *Commercial project management: A guide for selling and delivering professional services*. New York: Taylor & Francis.

ICM.

Lowe, D. J. (2008). Preface. In D. Lowe, & R. Leiringer (Eds), *Commercial management of projects: Defining the discipline* (pp. i–ix). Oxford: John Wiley & Sons,.

Lowe, D. J. & Leiringer, R. (2005). Commercial management in project-based organisations. *Journal of Financial Management of Property and Construction, 10*(1), 3–18.

Lowe, D. & Leiringer, R. (Eds). (2008). *Commercial management of projects: Defining the discipline*. Oxford: John Wiley & Sons.

PMI. (2017).

Turner, J. R. (1995). *The commercial project manager. Managing owners, sponsors, partners, supporters, stakeholders, contractors and consultants*. Maidenhead: McGraw Hill.

COMMERCIAL PROJECT MANAGEMENT: EXPANDS THE BODY OF KNOWLEDGE INTO AN ESSENTIAL DOMAIN

Robin Hornby

Introduction

Most of my career in IT and software development has been spent with vendors – migrating from an emphasis on hardware, to software, then to services as the decades passed. Services were really always a part of it, usually bundled, but the reality of managing a delivery team where real dollars are being consumed against a fixed project budget only struck home when I joined a dedicated contracting outfit in the early 1980s. There I started to experience the unique problems faced both by vendor project managers (PMs) and, increasingly, by PMs operating under commercial terms or constraints, as encountered in larger corporations operating an internal economy.

These problems fall into two general and related categories. The first is the lack of standards and the need that arises for an extension to the body of knowledge, not supplied by current offerings such as the Project Management Body of Knowledge (PMBOK®, PMI, 2017) or PRINCE2® (Axelos, 2017). The second category arises from the multiple views of project management (client, prime and subcontractors) that inevitably exist in this environment. This demands flexibility from the vendor, who must adapt to the client (more often than vice versa) and who is also faced with the need for internal (vendor) management discipline.

This has spawned a number of potential failure causes uniquely observed in the commercial project environment – poor integration as exhibited by project 'silos', poor recognition of the business role of PMs, poor connection between sales commitments and delivery capability, futile generation of multiple charters when really only one project is operating, poor project management communication, plummeting client satisfaction and narrow or disappearing vendor margins.

Overview of the situation

The introduction of a business relationship between a services firm, its project manager and a sponsor who is now a customer has a salutary effect on the traditional project management role. Project managers with little experience in these situations manage less effectively, jeopardising customer satisfaction and project profitability. At the same time, executives or owners of the firm are often unfamiliar with the disciplines of project management, especially at an early stage of their firm's evolution, so their support for a struggling project manager is lacking and the firm may never gain the foundation for healthy growth or even survival.

My generalised observations are as follows.

*   PMs lack experience and knowledge of business essentials, fail to run their projects as profit centres, and have difficulty understanding that their sponsor is also their customer; and
*   business owners are unaware of the potential for project management disciplines to enhance their business operations and are missing opportunities to gain much-needed business control.

Firms that have primed their PMs with business acumen and balanced an enthusiastic and skilful sales team with delivery management disciplines are rewarded with both successful projects and repeat business, which is the secret of a firm's profitability and longevity.

This, of course, is easier said than done. The essence of the problem is the inevitable encroachment of business management demands into the exclusive realm of project management. The PM requires training, proper exposure to legitimate vendor interests (and sometimes an attitude adjustment) to be successful.

The intersection between business and vendor project management can be expressed in three simple terms:

1   customer satisfaction and repeat business;
2   employee skill, growth and retention; and,
3   profit.

Contemplate the advice I received from a boss at my old consulting company, who had a unique way of emphasising these three priorities of the professional services firm: 'Success in this business is like juggling three balls: the profit, the customers, and the employees. If you drop one, I am not so interested in which one you dropped; just don't drop any!'

Resistance to process

In the minds of many managers, project management is synonymous with process, process and more process. Regrettably, implementing process as a driver of business success has been out of fashion since the late 1990s and the bursting of the great quality bubble. The current trend seems to downplay or even marginalise process, with the focus being on creativity and haste, freeing the talented employee from any form of discipline, and promoting results (what kind of results?) and a satisfied customer (for how long?) ahead of adherence to procedure. These are tempting options for the services firm that finds processes unappealing and relies instead on its above-average talent. They find reassurance in Tom Peters' infamous line in *The Pursuit of WOW!* where Peters quotes his colleague Richard Buetow who ironically suggested that a manufacturer of concrete lifejackets could be ISO certified so long as they were made following documented procedures and the next of kin were given instructions on how to complain about defects. I don't believe Peters was arguing against process, but he was instead pleading for balance between freedom to innovate and business discipline.

Although talent in business is needed, there aren't enough talented people to go around, and even if there were, building a business totally dependent on superior people is at best a short-term strategy and at worst a recipe for disaster. The majority of long-term successful businesses are dependent on the application of intelligent process. This must also apply to the professional services business.

Having argued that more is needed, be cautioned that distributing a procedures manual to all and sundry is not going to work. Firms are essentially entrepreneurial and sales people are instinctively hunters. A delicate touch must be applied, ensuring that formalisation is genuinely needed and can be appreciated by those who might resist. As the reader will discover, I generally avoid prescribing procedures and instead discuss practices (perhaps best practices), which leave more fluidity in the implementation than procedures, and can be supported by a loosely coupled variety of techniques and checklists.

Project management standards have limits

There are two dominant standards in the world today: the PMBOK® and PRINCE2®. Both are now widely implemented, but PMBOK® had its origins in the US and Canada, where it is prevalent, whereas PRINCE2® was developed in the UK and is stronger in Europe.

PMBOK® process groups show a sequential flow from initiation through a cyclic process of planning and executing, ending with closing. Monitoring and controlling is represented as a process group overarching all others. Procurement is described as a knowledge area, although purely as a buyer process executed as part of the client's existing project.

An unfortunate side-effect of the process group representation is that the groups are widely misinterpreted as part of a project life cycle, even though the PMBOK® states that process groups are not project phases. It appears to be a hybrid, caught between sequential phases such as initiation and closing, and repetitive functions such as planning, executing and controlling.

Both parties flounder with PMBOK® when the concept of a contract is introduced. It appears as though a new project is beginning and should go through initiation, but this cannot be true, as the project must already exist or there would be no procurement. Important preliminary deliverables such as the charter become ambiguous, with no clear ownership.

Adherence to the PMBOK® process group cycle almost encourages the emergence of a new project every time a procurement is launched. Essential unity is lost, and the silo effect between the vendor team and the client team can become dominant.

PRINCE2® is based on eight interacting high-level processes including directing, start–up, initiating, planning, controlling a stage, managing delivery, managing stage boundaries and closing. There are also eight components that can interact with all of the project management processes.

The major difficulty is that procurement is omitted from the scheme. This is explicitly acknowledged in the standard, with the assumption that the PM, and presumably the team, already exist on contract, or alternately exist in-house. The buyer and seller processes to get to this point are absent. It is not improbable to imagine an extension to these processes, and components that might accommodate buyer and seller activities to bid and execute a scope of work (or 'work package'), but at present they are not there.

The way forward

I have come to several conclusions when wrestling with these existing standards and how they might assist the goal of achieving wholesome integration between client and vendor project teams, and the need to bring structure to the fluid world of professional services.

The first conclusion is that imposing an operational standard on project management is counterproductive. Although standards have many benefits and over the past 20 years have resulted in appreciation and respect for the PM role, they have unfortunately contributed to the perception that project management exists in its own universe and is disconnected from the work of the project. The work of the project is expressed in a technique called the project life cycle (aka the application life cycle or the development life cycle), and it is time to put project management back where it belongs – integrated with the actual work.

Another conclusion is that implementing the minutiae of process in a mixed team and between managers from different organisations is next to impossible. Things need to be defined and agreed, but at a different level. Thus, specifying project management in terms of process, other than for those fundamentals called the core processes, is an uphill struggle. A much more productive view of the PM job, especially in the commercial world, is to see it as a set of functions. There are four – plan, organise, control and lead, sometimes abbreviated as POCL. These functions interact with the people and their organisations to get the work done.

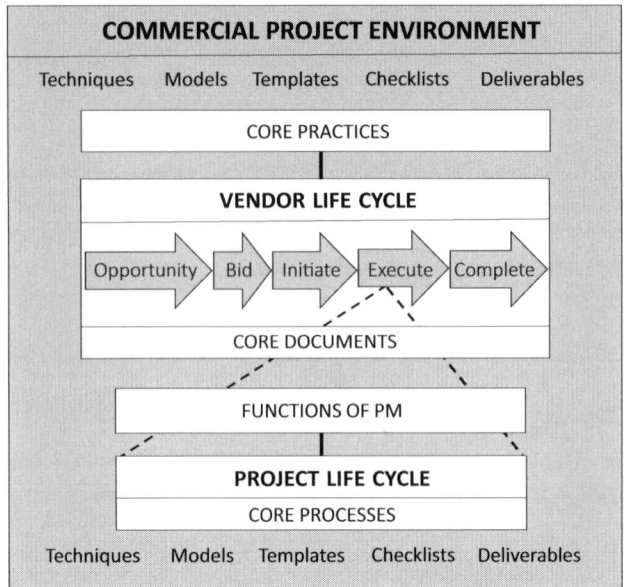

FIGURE 9.1 Architecture of the Commercial Project Environment (CPE)

A final conclusion is that really nothing in the standards addresses the reality of the vendor's role in the bidding and delivery of projects to the client's order. A framework is needed; project management's favourite technique comes to the rescue again and offers us a life cycle for vendors – opportunity, bid, initiate, execute and complete. Just as with the project life cycle, practices borrowed from project management can be applied to this life cycle as well, to provide business and risk management of the contract and get the job done.

An integrated solution summary, or commercial project environment (CPE) architecture diagram in Figure 9.1, clearly features the three concepts crystallised from my conclusions: a project life cycle; a vendor (or contract) life cycle; and functions of PM.

Recognition of two critical life cycles

The project life cycle describes the project work. A generic example might include phases for requirements, design, build, test, and implementation. The project life cycle is managed by applying the four functions of PM, and a small set of core processes. The vendor life cycle (sales and delivery) is supported by a set of core documents and practices. The execute phase provides for internal vendor management of the contracted phases of the project life cycle, as shown by the dashed lines. In the ecology are an array of techniques, deliverables and so forth, to be employed as needed.

The complexities of vendor project management are much simplified by this application of the life cycle technique. The vendor's need to bid, and then manage the contract to yield a profit, is based largely on vendor-confidential data and is satisfied by an internal contract life cycle. The customer's need to see the work of the project managed and executed in terms which they understand is the intent of a shared project life cycle. Attempting to bend one or the other to meet both purposes is unrealistic and disruptive.

I hope that the reader is persuaded by my conclusion, and perhaps their own experience, that working with the standard frameworks on a contracted project is an exercise in frustration, and there is little to support the vendor. A custom architecture, as presented, is the most productive solution. But the baby is not going out with the bathwater. Under the covers, most elements of sound project management are the same. Practices, techniques, checklists and deliverables are shamelessly taken from the standards, adapted and enhanced to meet our needs. They are then packaged into a more useful framework.

The functions of project management

My preference for representing project management as a set of functions, not a set of processes, and certainly not a life cycle, has been influenced by a definition of project management that impressed me many years ago. It is not in any standard literature that I can recall, but here it is and I commend it.

> Project management is a structured approach to plan, organise, control and lead the work of the project to meet project objectives.

Using this definition, the work of the project is organised (structured) into a life cycle and the work of the project manager is characterised as four functions. The definition does not mention deliverables, though the project manager accomplishes many of her functions through the production of deliverables. To firmly bring project management into reality, these deliverables should also be considered as 'work of the project' and integrated with the project life cycle and not hived off into some theoretical project management structure. This practice is called life cycle mapping.

A project life cycle aggregates project activities into sequential phases where each phase is distinctive in terms of the work being done by the team and the deliverables being produced. The work of the PM, on the other hand, is embodied in the functions of planning, organising, controlling and leading. These are repetitive and never-ending, as shown in Figure 9.2, and must not be confused

Plan, Organize, Control, and Lead

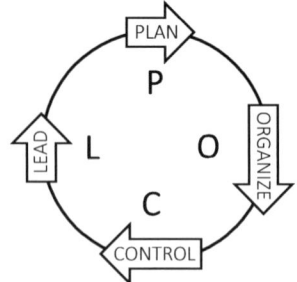

FIGURE 9.2 The four functions of project management (POCL)

with the sequential, phased work defined by the project life cycle and set in place by the project manager to guide the team.

Another way of thinking about the concept of project management functions during the project life cycle is to envision the project manager as continuously juggling her daily duties between POCL functions. Obviously, the emphasis placed on a specific function depends upon the deliverables being worked and the current phase situation. If the project is wrapping up a requirements phase and a project plan is being prepared, then the bulk of the day goes to planning, with the occasional hour or two on organising. But the next day may bring a working session with the sponsor where it is discovered that expectations are misaligned and departments have conflicting objectives. Now is the time for the project manager to show leadership. In due course, plans are baselined and the emphasis moves to controlling, but details must still be worked and variances resolved, so a day or two each week still goes to planning.

We now have the essential platform elements for commercial practice development. To recap: the establishment and general exposition of a universal project management model that fits client and vendor needs; the explicit adoption by client and vendor of a shared project life cycle into which everyone's deliverables are mapped; and the policy of the vendor to view contract management as a diciplined life cycle and not just a signing event. Practices developed on this platform, described in *Commercial Project Management*, address many of the failure causes uniquely observed in the commercial project environment.

Towards collaborative procurement of services

A natural extension of this discourse on vendor methods is a vision for full collaboration – a rational, collaborative procurement and delivery methodology – in which buyer and seller work together to optimise the results for both parties. The premise is that a new foundation must be laid.

Problems in the marketplace

Currently, buyers and sellers tend to operate as silos, creating communication tangles and misunderstandings, unnecessary complexity and sometimes causing project failures. Procurement, as generally understood by clients, is almost entirely focused on the selection and contracting of the vendor firm. The actual delivery of the project, which is surely the real goal of procurement, is left to oversight by a steering committee, and maybe occasional audits by the procurement department. Paradoxically, although sceptical buyers might feel otherwise, my case histories suggest that more savings will accrue to buyers than vendors if a collaborative approach is adopted. One area overlooked in such assessments is the frequent over-dependence on the vendor. Buyers tend not to properly examine methods used by their vendor, often fail to ask for meaningful status, fail to train their own staff, delegate the vendor to deal with risk and quality and often by default let the vendor PM entirely drive the project.

Total collaborative procurement (TCP)

A common framework that supports a collaborative approach would eliminate many direct and indirect costs for both parties and create a more effective project environment. It would vastly improve communications by jointly establishing a set of ground rules and practices to guide the parties through procurement, project execution and completion.

The vendor life cycle, merged with the buyer's procurement phase(s), is an obvious starting point to bring the vendor and client together at the business level in the same way as the shared project life cycle brings project management together at the PM level. The main challenge is to offer collaboration at the front end, where scope, estimates, risk and quality might be uncertain or ambiguous, whilst at the same time maintaining a fair and competitive environment.

A TCP architecture, perhaps ultimately developed, maintained and administered by a third party, includes a description of five joint phases and six joint practices. It is a significant adaptation of the CPE to support a collaborative approach. It eliminates the current inefficiencies but still permits a fair and competitive environment. Using the qualifier 'total' is a reminder that successful procurement is much more than just getting a qualified vendor selected for the project. Success demands that the entire delivery cycle is addressed. The client must abandon the idea that all risks and problems are delegated to the vendor. Projects are always a joint endeavour.

To bring this vision to reality will require considerable effort. The hope is that the productivity benefits, potentially of national significance, are recognised and the opportunity seized.

References

APM. (2012). *APM Body of Knowledge* (6th ed.). Princes Risborough, UK: Association of Project Management.

Axelos (2017). *Managing successful projects with PRINCE2.* (6th ed.). London: The Stationery Office.

ICM (2017). *The Institute of Commercial Management.* Ringwood, UK: Institute of Commercial Management.

PMI. (2017). *A guide to the project management body of knowledge* (6th ed.). Newton Square, PA: Project Management Institute.

CONCLUSION: RESPONDING TO THE CHALLENGE OF CHANGE

Darren Dalcher

Project work appears to be thriving in most sectors and domains. It underpins development and growth, as well as the implementation of policy, and hence carries strategic consequences. Yet, practitioners are searching for new types of answers that extend beyond the traditional techniques and approaches.

The chapters in this volume have brought together a range of ideas and solutions from varied contexts, merging and blending diverse approaches to project work. Looking across the entire collection, certain themes appear to emerge consistently, namely, people, context, strategy, governance and change.

People are everywhere within and around the project space. They lead, perform and engage with projects whose outcomes are designed for the needs of stakeholders. Scientific management, the root of most managerial approaches, was obsessed with efficiency, consequently eschewing participants and abrogating all decisions to the newly formed management cadre, resulting in an unmotivated and deskilled workforce. Production first, people second approaches can no longer work for knowledge workers and connected participants. Instead, in order to enable collaboration, managers have to project a positive image in order to influence the psychological environment in the workplace. Requirements management similarly begins with understanding, formulating and documenting the needs, wants and wishes of relevant stakeholders: individuals, groups, organisations and communities. Successful projects depend on trust as the essential glue ingredient for communication, relationships and collaboration; yet to trust someone inevitably implies taking a calculated risk. Leadership and engagement therefore remain crucial to building coalitions that will support organisational objectives and be alert and responsive to needs and expectations.

Contexts colour and shape every thing we see and do. Uncertain and unexpected contexts require greater adaptation and responsiveness, making judgement critical to improvement and survival. Moreover, the turbulence in some environments requires anti-fragile qualities, offering the requisite flexibility to continue to function and even improve their resilience through stress. Contexts also apply to individuals. Reflective practitioners recognise the limitations of instrumental methods and build on their experiences to derive enhanced understanding and new models that integrate new thinking and approaches that are both relevant and applicable. Stakeholders invoke different sets of concerns, requiring recognition of their specific viewpoints and expectations. In order to resolve ethical conflicts it is important to proactively share through multiple perspectives so as to appreciate the true complexity of ethical consideration. The poor track record of project delivery can be improved by addressing the commercial concerns related to the context of projects.

Strategy is closely entwined with execution, requiring an adaptive mind-set that is able to overcome difficulties and hurdles. Strategic initiatives translate organisational strategy into results through the action programmes needed to execute and realise the strategy. Projects are often carried out for strategic purposes, and the use of adaptive, responsive or anti-fragile approaches plays a key part in sustaining progress and exploiting emergent opportunities.

Governance refers to the control, influence and regulation required to conduct policy and action and secure the conditions needed to organise and steer both power and actions. Governance offers a language and a frame of reference. It can become unwieldy and overly restrictive, so in establishing effective governance systems there needs to be an appreciation of the value of 'good enough' governance that allows adaptation and responsiveness to observed conditions and impacts. Established frameworks enable alignment of objectives and relationships as well as control gates and formal roles. Delivering on business needs and expectations requires a strategic framework that allows project performance to be measured, reviewed and audited. The key to sustained excellence lies in the constant and continuous improvement and strategic direction that allow organisations to perform, adjust and reflect as part of their continuous improvement journey. Performance audits can then be used in adaptive fashion to reduce risk, enable transparency and create a culture of organisational maturity. Commercial management can be utilised to manage the relationships with external partners, as well as the links with the context and the wider environment. In particular, the vendor's role in the bidding and delivery of projects needs to be addressed through frameworks that accommodate the full life cycle, from opportunity to completion. A total collaborative procurement framework could be utilised to link vendor and clients in order to improve communication, coordinate processes and improve execution.

Change provides an opportunity to learn, rethink and reflect. It affords an impetus for evaluating the effectiveness of how things get done, but more importantly it helps to mark the point where significant transformation can be utilised to derive greater benefits. Change represents an improvement process rather than an event. In many initiatives, the key challenge is to alter people's behaviour and habit, as well as to deliver a structure or system. Ultimately, many of the causes of failed change initiatives revolve around change leaders who think that announcing change is sufficient, concerns that are never surfaced or addressed and those implementing change not being involved in the planning. Understanding the impact and scope of change is critical to success and requires consideration of leadership, culture, behaviours, capabilities and values. In fact, the success of many initiatives depends on the actual usage of their deliverables and on changes of behaviours that extend beyond traditional project parameters.

The themes offer a useful way of summarising the key messages from this collection. None the less, some of the themes appear to be interrelated. For example, change focuses on stakeholders and strategic understanding. Some themes appear to invoke others, as governance relies on standards and may consider stakeholders (people).

There are two additional related themes that seem to repeat across the set of themes. First, the need to *adapt, adjust and respond* seems to apply within most of the specific themes. In a world rife with turbulence and uncertainty, detailed plans and deliberate strategies seem inadequate as leaders recognise flexibility, resilience, diversity and anti-fragility as the measures of continuous capability. Second, many of the specific discussions imply *longer-term considerations and impacts* rather than a limited interest in short-term or immediate results. The longer-term interest makes sense, especially as organisations and leaders seek to adapt and respond and thereby develop *sustainable and enduring capabilities*.

The authors of the individual chapters appear to recognise that change can be frightening. Yet they also seem to respond to the opportunities of importing and sharing new perspectives. Their writing is replete with new things to learn, new developments and approaches that can replace tired processes, and new suggestions to improve the way we work and the way we can court, exploit and benefit from change through enhanced ways for managing, leading, governing and directing projects.

INDEX

Printed in Great Britain
by Amazon

49458296R00115